Spanish

Learn Spanish for Beginners: A Simple Guide that Will Help You on Your Language Learning Journey

Contents

Introduction

¡Hola!

First of all, this is not yet another typical Spanish book; this is a whole journey into Spanish!

If you tried to learn through the classical grammar lessons that did not work, or if your Spanish app is teaching you stuff you will never use in real life, this book is for you.

You will start from scratch and work your way from zero to fluent in 33 lessons where you will learn the basics of everyday Spanish—the real stuff that you will need when you go on a trip to South America or Spain.

There will be some grammar rules, but nothing boring and hard to memorize. The rules are threaded throughout the lessons to make it light and fun. You will move forward with real-life dialogues, stories, and practical examples that will make things easier and more entertaining.

Why learn Spanish? Well, if you are here already, you probably have your reasons. But maybe there are more reasons that you have not thought about...

Spanish is the official language of twenty countries. Around 400 million people speak it! Not only is it one of the most spoken

languages in the world, but Spanish is also one of the most studied…
by you and many others like you!

And it can be a real asset—since so many people speak and study the
language nowadays, even in the corporate and academic worlds. On
top of that, having friends in Latin America or Spain is something
you will never regret if you love travelling.

Once you are fluent in Spanish, you will find a door to a whole new
cultural world. For example, you will be able to read books in
Spanish that are not yet translated to your language, or you will be
able to pop into any cinema in Latin America and enjoy a good local
movie without subtitles.

Through these 33 short lessons, this book will not only teach you the
rules of Spanish grammar and vocabulary, but it will give you a
sense of the soul and music of the Spanish language. You will have a
solid beginner's foundation of Spanish, with phrases you can use to
navigate social situations and help you make friends and
connections.

Learning a language is a complex and rich experience. After you are
done with this book, you will be ready to travel, immerse yourself in
the Spanish-speaking cultures, read fiction and newspapers in
Spanish, watch films, eat Latin American and Spanish food and learn
the recipes, make Spanish-speaking friends, and, most importantly,
enjoy yourself! This book is inspiring and vibrant to read and listen
to, motivating you to speak and embrace the Spanish language, no
matter how new you are to it.

The first rule here is: do not be afraid. Spanish is much easier than it
seems!

¡Buena suerte!

Lesson 1

Vowels

The first thing you need to know if you want to learn Spanish is pronunciation.

This book will not drive you crazy with phonetic symbols and crazy rules; it will just show you the basic Spanish sounds with similar sounds in English. If you have heard Spanish before, you might know where this is heading already. Otherwise, do not panic! Spanish pronunciation is straightforward and does not change much. The Spanish alphabet contains 27 letters, most of which are pronounced *only one way*.

This does not happen in some other languages, like English or French. For example, think of how different the letter *e* sounds in *English* and in *elephant*. In French, there are five ways of pronouncing *e*. Spanish is the opposite: *e* is always pronounced the same.

There are a few exceptions, of course, but they are not complicated to remember—since they are quite similar in English.

On the other hand, Spanish pronunciation might be a bit tricky since there are so many Spanish-speaking countries and thus pronunciation varies quite a bit among them (mainly when it comes to vowels).

Of course, this book will teach you 'neutral' Spanish and will point out some big differences you might find from country to country, so you will be ready to talk your way through Latin America and Spain!

Vowels (vocales)

Let's start with the vowels.

They are the same as in English: *a, e, i, o, u*.

They are pronounced: *ah, eh, ee, oh, oo*.

Letter *a* is always pronounced like the *a* in *apricot*.

You can practice this sound in words like *casa* (*house*), *paz* (*peace*), and *mamá* (*mom*).

Letter *e* is always pronounced like the *e* in *elephant*.

You can practice this sound in words like *verde* (*green*), *pez* (*fish*), and *bebé* (*baby*).

Letter *i* always sounds like the *i* in *intelligence* or the *ee* in *meet* (when it is stressed).

You can practice this sound in words like *inglés* (*English*), *argentino* (*Argentinian*) or *salir* (*to go out*).

Letter *o* always sounds like the *o* in *tongue*.

You can practice this sound in words like *tomate* (*tomato*), *lobo* (*wolf*), and *loco* (*crazy*).

Letter *u* always sounds like the *oo* in *pool* or the English *w* in *water*.

You can practice this sound in words like *luna* (*moon*), *ducha* (*shower*), and *duda* (*doubt*).

Now, let's get all those example words and use them in simple sentences, so you can practice your pronunciation!

Do not worry; you are provided with the English translation of the sentence, and you can always go back if you feel like you are getting lost.

Letter *a*

The house is white – La casa es blanca

Alba loves peace – Alba ama la paz

Ana's mom is tall – La mamá de Ana es alta

Letter *e*

The boat is green – El bote es verde

The fish is thirsty – El pez tiene sed

The baby does not want milk – El bebé no quiere leche

Letter *i*

Tim is English – Tim es inglés

Martín is Argentinian – Martín es argentino

Irma wants to go out dancing – Irma quiere salir a bailar

Letter *o*

I have eight red tomatoes – Tengo ocho tomates rojos

The wolves are white –– Los lobos son blancos

The doctor is crazy – El doctor está loco

Letter *u*

The moon is dark – La luna está oscura

May I use your shower? – ¿Puedo usar tu ducha?

Tell me your doubt – Dime tu duda

Now you are going to be introduced to someone special. You will meet him a lot throughout this book. His name is James Dawkins, and he is quite lovely. He wants to see the world and become a travel journalist…

But first, he has to practice his Spanish! To do this, he bought a plane ticket from London to Cartagena, Colombia, and he is planning on traveling around South America.

The first person James talks to in South America is the woman behind the information desk at the airport. He has no internet coverage, so Google Maps is not an option, and he wants to know how to get to the hostel where he booked a bed. Luckily, he wrote the hostel's address on a piece of paper before taking off.

Let's practice the pronunciation of the vowels you just learned with this simple conversation:

JAMES: Hello! – ¡Hola!

WOMAN: Good morning – Buen día

JAMES: How can I go to this address? – ¿Cómo puedo ir a esta dirección?

WOMAN: You have to go outside and take bus number seven – Debes ir afuera y tomar el bus número siete.

JAMES: Great – Genial

WOMAN: You have to get off at the Centenario park – Debes bajar en el parque Centenario

JAMES: Do you have a map? – ¿Tiene un mapa?

WOMAN: Yes! Right here – ¡Sí! Aquí.

JAMES: Excellent. Thanks a lot. Have a good day – Excelente. Muchas gracias. Tenga un buen día.

Lesson 2

Consonants

Okay, vowels were easy, right? Well, get happier—because consonants are even easier! In most cases, they are the same as in English, only a bit softer.

Letter *b* in Spanish is similar to letter *b* in English, but while in English it sounds harder when it is at the beginning of a word (as in *beautiful*), in Spanish, it is always a soft sound (as in *cabin*).

You can practice this sound in words like *bebé* (*baby*), *abuelo* (*grandfather*), and *bonito* (*pretty*).

Letter *d* in Spanish is similar to *d* in English (as in *daisy*) but slightly softer.

You can practice this sound in words such as *dedo* (*finger*), *cuadrado* (*square*), and *dinosaurio* (*dinosaur*).

Letter *f* in Spanish sounds like *f* in English, in words such as *fish*.

You will find this sound in Spanish words like *feliz* (*happy*), *café* (*coffee*), and *fuego* (*fire*).

Letter *h* in Spanish is mute.

You will normally find it at the beginning of words, such as *hielo* (*ice*) or *huevo* (*egg*), but it can also be in the middle, as in *almohada* (*pillow*). The only situation where *h* has a sound is in combination with *c*, as in *chocolate* (*chocolate*).

Letter *j* in Spanish sounds like the Spanish *g* before letters *e* and *i*.

This means it sounds slightly harder than English *h* in words like *heaven*. You can find this letter in words such as *jamón* (*ham*), *jefe* (*boss*), and *joven* (*young*).

Letter *k* is not used in many words in Spanish, but you can find it in some like *kilo* (*kilo*) and *kiosco* (*kiosk*).

The sound is the same as the sound of letter *c* when it comes before letters *a*, *o*, *u* and consonants, as in *cantar* (*to sing*).

Letter *m* in Spanish always sounds like the *m* in English, as in *monster*. You can find this letter in words like *miedo* (*fear*) or *mejor* (*better*).

Letter *n* in Spanish always sounds like the *n* in English, as in *nonsense*. You can find this letter in words like *nunca* (*never*) or *nada* (*nothing*).

Letter *p* in Spanish sounds softer than the English *p*. It is actually more similar to the English *b* in *because*. You can find this sound in words like *perro* (*dog*) or *rápido* (*fast*).

Letter *s* always sounds like the *s* in *snake*.

You will use this sound in words like *silla* (*chair*) or *sol* (*sun*).

Letter *t* sounds stronger than American *t* and a little bit softer than British *t*.

You will use this sound in words like *tomate* (*tomato*) and *techo* (*roof*).

Letter *v* sounds similar to English *v*, maybe a little bit softer and sometimes not really different to *b* (a really normal mistake when writing in Spanish is to mix *b* and *v*).

You will find this sound in words like *vaca* (*cow*) and *vaso* (*glass*).

Letter *w* is not really common in Spanish, though it is included in the Spanish alphabet. It is only used in words with a foreign origin, like those that come from English.

It is pronounced like the English *w*, and you will find it in words like *kiwi* and *show*, which mean the same as in English.

Letter *x* is also not really common in Spanish, but it is used more than *k* and *w*. It sounds like a strong *c* and an *s* put together, just like in English. You will use it in words like *taxi* (*taxi*) and *conexión* (*connection*).

Letter *z* is pronounced, in some countries, like an *s*; but in some others, like Spain, it sounds similar to the *th* in *with* or *throne*. You will use the *z* in words like *cazar* (*to hunt*) and *zorro* (*fox*).

Now, let's use all these words in simple sentences!

Letter *b*

The baby is good – El bebé es bueno

My grandfather has a beard – Mi abuelo tiene barba

Your balcony is very pretty – Tu balcón es muy bonito

Letter *d*

I have ten fingers – Tengo diez dedos

Two golden squares – Dos cuadrados dorados

Where's the dinosaur? – ¿Dónde está el dinosaurio?

Letter *f*

Francisco is happy – Francisco está feliz

The coffee is very strong – El café está muy fuerte

In the end, there will be fireworks – Al final, habrá fuegos artificiales

Letter *h*

We need ice – Necesitamos hielo

The tortilla requires six eggs – La tortilla precisa seis huevos

I want another pillow – Quiero otra almohada

Letter *j*

Ham is typical from Spain – El jamón es típico de España

My boss is a really kind person – Mi jefe es una persona muy amable

You are very young – Eres muy joven

Letter *k*

A kilo of cheese, please – Un kilo de queso, por favor

Is there a kiosk around here? – ¿Hay un kiosco por aquí?

Letter *m*

Monsters frighten me – Los monstruos me dan miedo

I feel much better – Me siento mucho mejor

Letter *n*

I have never eaten oranges – Nunca he comido naranjas

Nothing is better than swimming – Nada es mejor que nadar

Letter *p*

My dog loves chasing balls – Mi perro ama perseguir pelotas

Pedro runs fast – Pedro corre rápido

Letter *s*

The chair is pink – La silla es rosa

The sun is rising! – ¡Sale el Sol!

Letter *t*

I have three tomatoes – Tengo tres tomates

The ball is on top of the roof – La pelota está sobre el techo

Letter *v*

The cow is old – La vaca está vieja

The glass is green – El vaso es verde

Letter *w*

I want a kilo of kiwis – Quiero un kilo de kiwis

When is the show starting? – ¿Cuándo empieza el show?

Letter *x*

Let's take a taxi – Tomemos un taxi

I have lost my internet connection – He perdido la conexión a internet

Letter *z*

It is forbidden to hunt – Está prohibido cazar

Foxes are beautiful – Los zorros son hermosos

Lesson 3

More Consonants

In the last chapter, consonants were stated as being easy... but that is not *quite* the truth. In fact, you probably noticed that some of them were skipped. This was because they are a bit trickier than the ones you just learned.

But do not be afraid! If you have come this far, you can take on a few rules regarding pronunciation, right?

Letter *c* in Spanish, just as in English, can have three sounds:

> The first is like the *c* in *cut*. Letter *c* always sounds like this when it comes before letters *a*, *o*, *u* and consonants (except *h*), as in words like *cama* (*bed*), *cosa* (*thing*), and *cuento* (*tale*).

> The second *c* sound is the same as the *s* sound. It sounds like this when it comes before letters *e* and *i*, as in *cerilla* (*match*), *círculo* (*circle*) or *cien* (*a hundred*).

> The third sound is only possible when *c* comes before *h*. The combination of *c* and *h* sounds like the *ch* in *change*. You

will find it in words like *colchón* (*mattress*), *chocolate* (*chocolate*), and *chiste* (*joke*).

Letter g in Spanish can have a soft sound and a hard sound:

You get the soft g when it comes before letters *a*, *o*, *u* and consonants. In these cases, it sounds like English g in *green*. You can find this sound in words like *gato* (*cat*), *gusto* (*taste*), and *gracias* (*thanks*).

You also get this sound when you have the combination of letters *gue* and *gui*. In these cases, the *u* is not pronounced, just as it happens in English in *guest* or *guilty*. You can find this sound in Spanish in words such as *guerra* (*war*) and *guitarra* (*guitar*). The *u* is only pronounced when there is a diaeresis (two dots) on top of it, as in *pingüino* (*penguin*) or *antigüedad* (*antique*), but this is not very common.

The hard g sound in Spanish is similar to the *h* sound in the English word *helicopter*. You can find this sound when g comes before letters *e* and *i*, as in *gente* (*people*) or *girasol* (*sunflower*).

Letter l in Spanish sounds the same as letter *l* in English.

You can find it in words such as *limón* (*lemon*) or *loco* (*crazy*).

However, when two *l* are put together, the sound changes. The **ll** sounds different in different places. Depending on the country or region, it could be pronounced like the Spanish *i*, like the combination *li*, like the English *y* in *yellow*, like the *j* in *jello* or like the *sh* in *show*.

There is no 'right' way to pronounce it. If you are interested in going to one specific place, you can research how they pronounce it there; otherwise, you can pick your favorite!

You will find this combination of letters in words like *calle* (*street*), *pollo* (*chicken*), and *lluvia* (*rain*).

Letter ñ sounds like the combination of letters *ni*, as in *nibble*.

You can find this letter in words like *niño* (*kid*), where the *ni* and the *ñ* sounds are just the same. Other words with letter *ñ* are *contraseña* (*password*), *señal* (*signal*), and *dueño* (*owner*).

Letter *q* is only used in Spanish in the combinations *que* and *qui*. In these cases, the *u* is silent, and the *q* sounds like *c* when it comes before letters *a*, *o*, *u* and consonants.

You can find letter *q* in words like *queso* (*cheese*) and *quizás* (*maybe*).

Letter *r* has two different sounds in Spanish, a soft sound and a hard sound:

> The strong *r* sound is very difficult to non-Spanish speakers, so if you want to roll your *r* like a local, you need to try to place your tongue in the front of your palate, right behind your teeth and try to make air pass through until it sounds like a starting engine. You will need this sound for words that start with *r*, like *rata* (*rat*), and for words that have a double *r*, like *perro* (*dog*).

> When you are ready to roll your *r*, here is a very popular Spanish tongue-twister for you: *erre con erre guitarra, erre con erre carril, mira que rápido ruedan las rápidas ruedas del ferrocarril.*

> The soft *r* is easier, and it sounds like the American sound for *t* in *water*. You will use the soft *r* in words like *cara* (*face*), *toro* (*bull*), and *paraguas* (*umbrella*).

Letter *y* has two different sounds:

> It sounds like Spanish *i* (like the *i* in *intelligence* or the *ee* in *meet*) in words like *y* (*and*) or *hoy* (*today*).

> It can sound like Spanish *ll* and also sounds different in different Latin American countries and in Spain: it is pronounced like the Spanish *i*, like the English *y* in *yellow,*

the *j* in *jello*, or the *sh* in *show*. You will find it in really common words like *yo* (*I*) and *ya* (*now*).

Now let's practice with some real-life examples:

Letter *c*

Hard *c* sound:

I eat on the bed – Yo como en la cama

I believe in many things – Creo en muchas cosas

Tell me a story! – ¡Cuéntame un cuento!

Soft *c* sound:

Light the match – Enciende la cerilla

The circle is light blue – El círculo es celeste

I have a hundred bicycles – Tengo cien bicicletas

Ch sound:

There is gum on my mattress – Hay un chicle en mi colchón

There is chocolate on my vest – Hay chocolate en mi chaleco

The chef tells a joke – El chef cuenta un chiste

Letter *g*

Soft *g* sound:

The cat is nice – El gato es agradable

Nice to meet you! – ¡Mucho gusto!

Thank you very much – Muchas gracias

My grandfather went to the war – Mi abuelo fue a la guerra

Gabriel plays the guitar – Gabriel toca la guitarra

There are penguins in the south – Hay pingüinos en el sur

Hard *g* sound:

People are partying – La gente está de fiesta

It is sunflower oil – Es aceite de girasol

Letter *l*

Buy a lemon – Compra un limón

Lucas is crazy – Lucas está loco

Ll

The street is full of people – La calle está llena de gente

The chicken is very tasty – El pollo está muy sabroso

The rain is very strong – La lluvia es muy fuerte

Letter *ñ*

The kid is very little – El niño es muy pequeño

My password is secret – Mi contraseña es secreta

I have no phone signal – No tengo señal en el móvil

The restaurant's owner is very funny – El dueño del restaurante es muy gracioso

Letter *q*

I want cheese! – ¡Quiero queso!

Maybe nobody will want to go to the cinema – Quizá nadie quiera ir al cine

Letter *r*

Strong *r* sound:

Run! A rat! – ¡Corre, una rata!

Your dog is weird – Tu perro es raro

Soft *r* sound:

Your face is wonderful – Tu cara es maravillosa

Bulls suffer during bullfighting – Los toros sufren en las corridas

Bring an umbrella! – ¡Trae un paraguas!

Letter *y*

Vowel sound:

I am a musician and an actor – Soy músico y actor

Today I leave – Hoy me voy

Consonant sound:

I am called Lucía – Yo me llamo Lucía

We are going now – Ya estamos yendo

¡Genial!

Now you can do some Spanish pronunciation.

Yes, some of it is quite simple, but a few sounds are a bit more complicated (those rolling *rrrrrs* are something special, right?).

Do not worry too much about it—people will understand you even if the Spanish is not perfect.

Whenever you are talking with a Spanish native, try to listen carefully to the way they pronounce different words and do not be afraid to try to imitate them when it is your turn to speak. That is what good pronunciation is all about!

Watching movies and listening to songs in Spanish will also loosen up your ears and tongue. And you might get some cultural insights as well!

Lesson 4

Singular Personal Pronouns

If you want to learn Spanish, as soon as you can do some basic pronunciation, one of the first things you need to learn is *personal pronouns*.

This just means you have to learn how to say *I, you, we, she...* basic stuff! This is important because you need to be able to communicate with others—to say who you are, to ask questions about others, to make friends!

And that is one of the best things about traveling—people. There is no traveling without meeting people. Even if you are traveling on your own, you will definitely talk to many people at the hostel or hotel where you will stay, or maybe you are going to a conference and want to be able to talk to your colleagues. People are everywhere and, to be able to chat with them, *personal pronouns* are a must.

I – yo

you – tú

he – él

she – ella

we – nosotros/nosotras

you – vosotros/vosotras or ustedes

they – ellos/ellas

Yo

The first and most important pronoun you should learn in any language is how to say *I*. The Spanish word for *I* is *yo*.

Here are some sentences with the pronoun *yo*:

*I am Jake – **Yo** soy Jake*

*I come from Europe – **Yo** vengo de Europa*

*My name is Alicia – **Yo** me llamo Alicia*

So, to make things more interesting, imagine some real-world examples, so you can already picture traveling and speaking Spanish in your mind.

James is starting his year-round trip in South America. He arrives at his hostel in Cartagena, Colombia, and the first person he meets is the receptionist, Alicia, who says hello and wants to check him in:

ALICIA: Hello! What is your name? – ¡Hola! ¿Cómo te llamas?

*JAMES: I am James – **Yo** soy James*

*ALICIA: Welcome, James. I am Alicia. Where are you from? – Bienvenido, James. **Yo** soy Alicia. ¿De dónde eres?*

*JAMES: I am English – **Yo** soy inglés*

Tú

Let's move forward to *you*, which in Spanish is *tú*.

Here are some sentences with the pronoun *tú*:

*You are tall – **Tú** eres alto*

*You are Peruvian – **Tú** eres peruano*

*You have a beautiful house – **Tú** tienes una casa hermosa*

Let's go back to James. At the backpacker's hostel, he meets many lovely people. In the common lounge, he talks to a Colombian woman. Someone told him her name is María, but he is not sure, so he will try to ask:

*JAMES: Are you María? – ¿**Tú** eres María?*

*MARÍA: Yes, my name is María. What is your name? – Sí, mi nombre es María. ¿**Tú** cómo te llamas?*

*JAMES: I am James. Are you Colombian? – Soy James. ¿**Tú** eres colombiana?*

*MARÍA: Yes, I am Colombian. Are you English? – Sí, soy colombiana. ¿**Tú** eres inglés?*

JAMES: Yes! – ¡Sí!

Please note: For those who are interested in *writing* in Spanish, always remember to put the *tilde* on top of the *u* when you write *tú*. The tilde is the little mark on top of some vowels. If you write *tu*, without the *tilde*, it will be pronounced the same, but it will mean something different: it will mean *your*. In case you want to know more about how to use Spanish *tildes*, an annex is included that you can check!

Él

Now you can talk about yourself and the person in front of you. But what if you want to talk about a third person?

Just as in English, in Spanish, there is a word for *he* and another word for *she*.

The word for *he* is *él*.

Here are some sentences with the pronoun *él*:

*He has a good job – **Él** tiene un buen trabajo*

*He is hungry – **Él** tiene hambre*

*He loves traveling – **Él** ama viajar*

Back at the hostel in Colombia, and after chatting for some time, María asks James if he wants to meet her boyfriend:

*MARÍA: Do you want to meet my boyfriend? He is at the bookstore – ¿Quieres conocer a mi novio? **Él** está en la tienda de libros.*

*JAMES: Sure! What does he do for work? – ¡Claro! ¿De qué trabaja **él**?*

*MARÍA: He is an engineer – **Él** es ingeniero.*

*JAMES: Is he also Colombian? – ¿**Él** también es colombiano?*

*MARÍA: No, he is Australian – No, **él** es australiano.*

Please note: Just as with *tú*—for those who want to write good Spanish like the locals—always remember to put the *tilde* on top of the *e* when you write *él*. If you write *el*, without the *tilde*, it means something different: it means *the*.

Ella

Now, let's suppose you are talking about a woman or a girl.

The Spanish word for *she* is ***ella***.

Here are some sentences with the pronoun *ella*:

*She is a lawyer – **Ella** es abogada*

*She has a big house – **Ella** tiene una casa grande*

*She will have dinner with us – **Ella** cenará con nosotros*

Now, María and James leave the hostel and go to the bookstore to find María's boyfriend, Alex.

Even though Alex is Australian, they always speak in Spanish because they do not want to be rude to María, and, of course, because they want to practice and get better. That is why they are in Colombia, after all!

James and María say hello to Alex, and afterward, Alex explains why he is buying a book:

*ALEX: Do you know Alicia, the receptionist? It is her birthday. She is having a party – ¿Conoces a Alicia, la recepcionista? Es su cumpleaños. **Ella** hará una fiesta.*

*JAMES: Yes, she invited me. Did you buy something for her? – Sí, **ella** me ha invitado. ¿Le has comprado algo?*

ALEX: I bought her a book –- Le he comprado un libro.

*MARÍA: She loves books – **Ella** ama los libros.*

*JAMES: I know! She told me so – ¡Lo sé! **Ella** me lo dijo.*

Lesson 5

Plural Personal Pronouns

Nosotros and nosotras

If you are traveling alone, *yo* can be really useful. But what if you are with a group and you need to say *we*. Or maybe you are very social, like James, and you made a group of friends already?

In English, there are two different words for *he* and *she*, but there is only one for *we*. In Spanish, on the other hand, things are not so simple! There are two pronouns for *we*, one is masculine, and the other one is feminine: *nosotros* and *nosotras*.

So, if your group is male-only, you will use *nosotros*, and if you are a woman and talking about an all-female party, you will say *nosotras*.

What if three boys and one girl form your group? In that case, you will say *nosotros*. And if you are three girls and one boy, you will also say *nosotros*.

Even if there is only one male in a group of hundreds of females, the 'right' pronoun to use is *nosotros*. This is called the 'generic masculine'.

It might sound unfair, yet it is the way Spanish works… at least for now (people do want to change it so the rule might change in the future).

Let's read some examples!

Here are some sentences with the pronouns *nosotros* and *nosotras*:

*We come from New Zealand – **Nosotros** venimos de Nueva Zelanda*

*We have bought drinks! – ¡**Nosotros** hemos comprado bebidas!*

*We are the champions – **Nosotros** somos los campeones*

*We are going out for dinner – **Nosotras** vamos a ir a cenar afuera*

*We want to visit Chile – **Nosotras** queremos viajar a Chile*

*We are tired – **Nosotras** estamos cansadas*

Back in beautiful Cartagena, María and Alicia are planning on going to the local museum at Bolívar park. It is called Museo Histórico de Cartagena, and it is in the city's old Inquisition Palace. In the eighteenth century, it was where the Catholic Inquisition in Cartagena worked and even tortured people. María and Alicia ask James and Alex if they are going as well:

*MARÍA: We are going to the museum today – **Nosotras** vamos al museo hoy*

*JAMES: We as well, but first we are going to the park – **Nosotros** también, pero antes vamos a ir al parque*

*MARÍA: We went to the park yesterday – **Nosotras** fuimos al parque ayer*

*JAMES: We do not know it yet, is it nice? – **Nosotros** no lo conocemos aún, ¿es agradable?*

MARÍA: It is lovely! – ¡Es hermoso!

Vosotros/ustedes

Depending on if you travel to Latin America or Spain, you will find there are two different ways for the plural *you*: ***vosotros*** (Spain) and ***ustedes*** (Latin America). And the tricky part is that using one or the other changes the conjugation of the verbs.

Vosotros and *ustedes* will be explained separately now, and then, when talking about conjugations, both ways will be shown.

Vosotros, just like *nosotros*, has a feminine version. The same rules apply: when there is at least one male in the group, the masculine version is used: ***vosotros***. If it is an all-female group, then you should use ***vosotras***.

Here are some sentences with the pronouns *vosotros* and *vosotras*:

You are the best – ***Vosotros*** *sois los mejores*

Are you cold? – *¿****Vosotros*** *tenéis frío?*

You cook very well – ***Vosotros*** *cocináis muy bien*

You love sports – ***Vosotras*** *amáis los deportes*

You are very tall – ***Vosotras*** *sois muy altas*

You are hungry – ***Vosotras*** *tenéis hambre*

After James and Alex walk around the park for some time, they meet María and Alicia near the museum:

ALICIA: Did you enjoy the park? – *¿****Vosotros*** *habéis disfrutado el parque?*

ALEX: Yes! What did you do? – *¡Sí! ¿****Vosotras*** *qué habéis hecho?*

ALICIA: We rested. Do you want to go to the museum now? – *Nosotras descansamos. ¿****Vosotros*** *queréis ir al museo ahora?*

ALEX: Yes! Sounds good. Do you have your tickets? – *¡Sí! Suena bien. ¿****Vosotras*** *tenéis vuestros billetes?*

MARÍA: Sure! – *¡Claro!*

Ustedes, on the other hand, has no masculine or feminine version. It is neutral. *However*, as you will see in some of these examples, you do have to use feminine or masculine articles and adjectives depending on the group.

Let's view the same sentences as before, but using *ustedes*:

You are the best – **Ustedes** son **los** mejores

Are you cold? – ¿**Ustedes** tienen frío?

You cook very well – **Ustedes** cocinan muy bien

You love sports – **Ustedes** aman los deportes

You are very tall – **Ustedes** son muy **altas**

You are hungry – **Ustedes** tienen hambre

Now let's review the same conversation, but using *ustedes* instead of *vosotros*.

After James and Alex walk around the park for some time, they meet María and Alicia near the museum:

ALICIA: Did you enjoy the park? – ¿**Ustedes** han disfrutado el parque?

ALEX: Yes! What did you do? – ¡Sí! ¿**Ustedes** qué han hecho?

ALICIA: We rested. Do you want to go to the museum now? – Nosotras descansamos. ¿**Ustedes** quieren ir al museo ahora?

ALEX: Yes! Sounds good. Do you have your tickets? – ¡Sí! Suena bien. ¿**Ustedes** tienen sus billetes?

MARÍA: Sure! – ¡Claro!

Tip: There is no need to go crazy with *ustedes/vosotros*. It is recommended that you learn *ustedes* if you want to go to Latin America and *vosotros* if you are more interested in Spain. Either way, people in Latin America will understand *vosotros* perfectly, and people in Spain can also understand *ustedes* (they even use it sometimes in really formal occasions).

Ellos y ellas

The last thing you need to learn is how to talk about groups of people.

Good things come in pairs! So just as there are the masculine and feminine pronouns *nosotros* and *nosotras*, and *vosotros* and *vosotras*, in Spanish, there are also two pronouns for *they*: **ellos** and **ellas**.

Again, if the group is male-only, you will use *ellos*, and if it is an all-female party, you will use *ellas*.

Let's see some examples!

Here are some sentences with the pronouns *ellos* and *ellas*:

*They are very funny – **Ellos** son muy divertidos*

*They are hungry – **Ellos** tienen hambre*

*They are Argentinians – **Ellos** son Argentinos*

*They are very smart – **Ellas** son muy inteligentes*

*They have loads of energy – **Ellas** tienen mucha energía*

*They are Chilean – **Ellas** son chilenas*

At the hostel in Cartagena, there are rooms for women and rooms for men. In the men's room, James and Alex are talking about Alicia and María. In the women's room, the girls are talking about James and Alex!

Let's see what they say about each other, starting with María and Alicia's room:

*MARÍA: I had a lot of fun with Alex and James today; they are great! – Me divertí mucho con Alex y James hoy; ¡**ellos** son geniales!*

*ALICIA: Yes, they are my favorite guests… besides you, of course – Sí, **ellos** son mis huéspedes preferidos… además de ti, claro*

*MARÍA: They want to go to the cinema tomorrow. Do you want to go? – **Ellos** quieren ir al cine mañana. ¿te apetece ir?*

Now let's see what the guys say:

*JAMES: It was a great day at the museum with María and Alicia. They make me laugh – Fue un buen día en el museo con María y Alicia. **Ellas** me hacen reir*

*ALEX: Me too! They should have a comedy show – ¡A mí también! **Ellas** deberían tener un show de comedia*

*JAMES: Maybe they can make a comedy show at the hostel – Quizá **ellas** pueden hacer un espectáculo de comedia en el hostal*

Lesson 6

Special Personal Pronouns

Usted and vos

Yes, there are still other pronouns; however, you only need to learn these for particular situations.

First of all, let's start with **usted**. *Usted* is *you*.

But if *tú* is *you*, then who is *usted*?

Actually, *usted* is the formal version of *you*. In some countries, it is more used than in others. It could be used to speak with strangers, older people, or people from work/university in formal settings.

The conjugation is super easy because it is the same as for *él/ella* (*he/she*).

Let's see some examples with *tú*, *él/ella* and *usted* so that you can see it clearly:

*You are tall – **Tú** eres alto*

*He is tall – **Él** es alto*

*You are tall – **Usted** es alto*

*You are Peruvian – **Tú** eres peruana*

*She is Peruvian – **Ella** es peruana*

*You are Peruvian – **Usted** es peruana*

*You have a beautiful house – **Tú** tienes una casa hermosa*

*He/she has a beautiful house – **Él/ella** tiene una casa hermosa*

*You have a beautiful house – **Usted** tiene una casa hermosa*

Vos is also *you*! You only should worry about *vos* if you are traveling to a specific region, such as Argentina, Uruguay, Paraguay, and some parts of other countries (like Medellín, in Colombia).

This pronoun uses a slightly different conjugation for most verbs. If you want to be understood in every Spanish-speaking country, though, learning the pronoun *tú* is more than enough. But if you want to, say, travel to Argentina and *understand* people, knowing a *vos* won't hurt.

Vos will be used in the book, in case you are traveling through some of the *vos* regions. For now, let's see a few examples of *tú* and *vos*:

*You are hungry – **Tú** tienes hambre*

*You are hungry – **Vos** tenés hambre*

*You are great – **Tú** eres genial*

*You are great – **Vos** sos genial*

*Do you come from Argentina? – ¿**Tú** vienes de Argentina?*

*Do you come from Argentina? – ¿**Vos** venís de Argentina?*

Lesson 7

The Icebreaker: Saying Hello

Naturally, the first thing you need to learn to engage in a conversation is how to say *hello*! So now you will learn all sorts of greetings and introductions.

Informal greetings

The very first word you will probably hear when traveling in Latin America or Spain is **hola**!

Hola is literally *hello*, and although it is mainly informal, you can use it in most situations. Remember the *h* is mute, so the right way to say *hola* is *oh-lah* (stressing the *oh* syllable).

Let's see some examples and go back to the hostel in Cartagena, where a group of four Mexican girls has just arrived:

JAMES: Hello! – ¡Hola!

SARA: Hello! – ¡Hola!

ALBA: Hello! – ¡Hola!

MARTA: Hello! – ¡Hola!

DANIELA: Hello! – ¡Hola!

You probably won't forget it now! Here are some other ways to greet someone:

Good morning – Buenos días

Good afternoon – Buenas tardes

Good evening – Buenas noches

How are you? – ¿Cómo estás?

What is up? – ¿Qué tal?

What is new? – ¿Qué hay de nuevo?

All good? – ¿Todo bien?

Very well! – ¡Muy bien!

I am well. How about you? – Yo estoy bien. ¿y tú?

Hello, everybody! – ¡Hola a todos!

Nice to see you! – ¡Qué gusto verte!

If you are greeting someone you have not met before, let's see what you need to know to get to know someone in Spanish:

Who are you? – ¿Quién eres?

What is your name? – ¿Cómo te llamas?

My name is – Mi nombre es / Me llamo

Where are you from? – ¿De dónde eres?

I am from – Soy de

I come from – Vengo de

How old are you? – ¿Cuántos años tienes?

What is your age? – ¿Cuál es tu edad?

What do you do for a living? – ¿A qué te dedicas?

Where do you work? – ¿Dónde trabajas?

What do you do for work? – ¿De qué trabajas?

What do you study? – ¿Qué estudias?

Let's try to put some of these greetings and introductory questions into simple sentences. So, after saying *hello*, James introduces himself to the Mexican girls, and they talk a bit about themselves:

JAMES: My name is James – Mi nombre es James

SARA: I am Sara. Where are you from? – Yo soy Sara. ¿De dónde eres?

JAMES: I am from England; I am English – Soy de Inglaterra; soy inglés

SARA: Oh, you are English? Where in England do you come from? – Oh, ¿eres inglés? ¿De dónde en Inglaterra?

JAMES: I am from Manchester, but I live in London now – Soy de Manchester, pero ahora vivo en Londres.

SARA: London is a beautiful city – Londres es una ciudad hermosa

JAMES: Do you know London? – ¿Conoces Londres?

SARA: Of course! It is one of my favourite cities – ¡Claro! Es una de mis ciudades favoritas

JAMES: What are your names, girls? – ¿Cuáles son vuestros nombres, chicas?

ALBA: Hello, James, I am Alba – Hola, James. Yo soy Alba

MARTA: I am Marta! – ¡Yo soy Marta!

DANIELA: My name is Daniela, but you can call me Dani – Mi nombre es Daniela, pero puedes llamarme Dani

JAMES: Okay, so it is Sara, Alba, Marta and... ¡Dani! Right? – Okay, entonces es Sara, Alba, Marta y... Dani, ¿verdad?

SARA, ALBA, MARTA AND DANIELA: Yes! – ¡Sí!

Formal greetings

Of course, not every situation is so informal as the hostel. What happens if you are in a formal context? Is it okay to address people as *tú*? The socially acceptable way to strangers, older people and people in general in a very formal professional or academic environment is to use *usted*.

To say *hello*, first of all, it is better in these situations to say *buenos días* (*good morning*) or *buenas tardes* (*good afternoon*) instead of *hola*. These are other greetings that you can use in a formal situation:

It is a pleasure to meet you – Es un placer conocerlo/conocerla

It is an honor to meet you – Es un honor conocerlo/conocerla

What is your name? – ¿Cómo se llama?

What is your name? – ¿Cuál es su nombre?

Where are you from? – ¿De dónde es?

What do you do for a living? – ¿A qué se dedica?

Where do you work? – ¿Dónde trabaja?

Shortly after the five Mexican girls go up to their room, another person walks into the hostel. By the way the staff talks to her, James realizes she is the owner of the place.

JAMES: Good morning! – ¡Buenos días!

ANDREA: Good afternoon, it is two already – Buenas tardes, ya son las dos

JAMES: Oh, I'm sorry – Oh, disculpe

ANDREA: Do not worry – No hay por qué

JAMES: Are you the hostel's owner? – ¿Es usted la dueña del hostal?

ANDREA: Yes! Me and my partner are the owners – ¡Sí! Yo y mi pareja somos las dueñas

JAMES: It is a pleasure to meet you. You have a beautiful hostel – Es un placer conocerla. Tiene un hermoso hostal

ANDREA: Thanks! You can refer to me as tú, *you know? – ¡Gracias! Puedes tutearme, ¿sabes?*

JAMES: Oh, okay: it is a pleasure to meet you – Ah, está bien: es un placer conocerte

There is a specific verb in the conversation, *tutear*, that means 'to use *tú* instead of *usted*'. In other words, if someone says *tutéame*, they mean 'there is no need to be so formal'.

Lesson 8

To Be or Not to Be: Basic Verbs

Now, before you move forward, let's use these pronouns you have just learned to study some basic verbs you will need in almost any conversation: *ser, estar, ir* and *tener*.

Of course, you will see only the present tense, for now, and thread them with some practical examples.

Just in case, an annex is included at the end of the book where you will find the conjugation for the most common verbs in Spanish in all tenses, so you can have a peek any time you are in trouble.

Ser and *estar*

The first verb you need to learn is *ser*, which is *to be*. This is necessary because you will use it any time you are talking about yourself or asking others who they are.

I am – yo soy

You are – tú eres / usted es / vos sos

He is – él es

She is – ella es

We are – nosotros somos / nosotras somos

You are – vosotros sois / vosotras sois / ustedes son

They are – ellos son / ellas son

Let's see how James does with the verb *ser*. He has just met the hostel's owner, Andrea:

*ANDREA: My name is Andrea. What's your name – Mi nombre **es** Andrea. ¿Cuál **es** tu nombre?*

*JAMES: I am James – Yo **soy** James*

*ANDREA: Oh, you are James! You are Alicia's friend, right? – Ah, ¡tú **eres** James! **Eres** el amigo de Alicia, ¿verdad?*

*JAMES: Yes! We met here some days ago, but we are friends already – ¡Sí! Nos conocimos aquí hace unos días, pero ya **somos** amigos*

*ANDREA: That accent is very particular, are you British? – Ese acento **es** muy particular, ¿**eres** británico?*

*JAMES: Yes, I am from England – Sí, **soy** de Inglaterra*

*ANDREA: That is great! You English people are the best – ¡Qué bien! Los ingleses **sois** lo máximo*

Now, you will learn the verb *estar*, which is… also *to be*!

You will learn how to use both verbs with practice, but the general rule is that *ser* is for permanent things:

*I am James – **Soy** James*

*I am English – **Soy** inglés*

*I am a journalist – **Soy** periodista*

On the other hand, *estar* is for temporary states, like feelings or locations:

*I am tired – **Estoy** cansado*

*I am in South America – **Estoy** en Sudamérica*

*I am learning Spanish – **Estoy** aprendiendo español*

This is the present tense conjugation for the verb *estar*:

I am – yo estoy

You are – tú estás / usted está / vos estás

He is – él está

She is – ella está

We are – nosotros estamos / nosotras estamos

You are – vosotros estáis / vosotras estáis / ustedes están

They are – ellos están / ellas están

James and Andrea talk a bit more about what they are doing in the present. Luckily for James, he knows the verb *estar* very well:

*ANDREA: Are you happy with your stay here? – ¿**Estás** contento con tu estadía aquí?*

*JAMES: Sure! The hostel is very good; I am happy here – ¡Claro! El hostal **está** muy bien; **estoy** feliz aquí*

*ANDREA: And we are happy to have you. What are you doing in Colombia? – I nosotros **estamos** felices de tenerte, ¿qué **estás** haciendo en Colombia?*

*JAMES: I am planning a year-round trip in South America; I am just starting – **Estoy** planeando un viaje de un año en Sudamérica; recién **estoy** comenzando*

*ANDREA: That is very good! – ¡Eso **está** muy bien!*

Ir

Another very important Spanish verb, especially if you love traveling, is *ir*, which is *to go*. Just like *ser* and *estar* it is an irregular verb, but you will use it so much that you will probably have no problems with it.

I go – yo voy

You go – tú vas / usted va / vos vas

He goes – él va

She goes – ella va

We go – nosotros vamos / nosotras vamos

You go – vosotros vais / vosotras vais / ustedes van

They go – ellos van / ellas van

Now you can see how simple English conjugations are in comparison with Spanish conjugations. In English, for every pronoun, except he/she, you just say *go*. Instead, in Spanish, there are so many words for it! The difference is that, in English, you *always* say the pronoun, while in Spanish, thanks to the different conjugations, you can just say the verb alone:

*I go to Colombia – **Voy** a Colombia*

*He goes to the library – **Va** a la biblioteca*

*We are going to dance! – ¡**Vamos** a bailar!*

While James and Andrea are chatting, Alex shows up at the living room and joins them:

*ALEX: Hi! I am going to the market; do you want something? – ¡Hola! **Voy** al Mercado; ¿queréis algo?*

*ANDREA: No, thanks. I am waiting for Alicia. We are going to a restaurant together – No, gracias. Estoy esperando a Alicia. **Vamos** a comer a un restaurante juntas*

*ALEX: James, are you going with them? – James, ¿tú **vas** con ellas?*

*JAMES: No, I am going to the beach. The day is going to be nice – No, **voy** a la playa. El día **va** a estar lindo*

As you can see, just as in English, Spanish uses the verb *ir (to go)* to talk about the future. This is the simpler form of the future, so if you can learn the verb *ir* in the present tense, you do not need to learn complicated future-tense conjugations:

Tomorrow I am going to your house – Mañana **voy** *a tu casa*

*Shall we go dancing this evening? – ¿***Vamos** *a bailar esta noche?*

The weather is going to be really rainy – El clima **va** *a estar muy lluvioso*

*Are you two having a baby? – ¿***Vais** *a tener un bebé?*

Tener

The last basic verb you need to learn is *tener*, which means *to have*.

In Spanish, just as in English, *tener* is used to talk about possessions:

I have a book – Tengo un libro

We have a double room – Tenemos una habitación doble

She has three siblings – Ella tiene tres hermanos

However, additionally, *tener* is used for age and some feelings. In English, you normally use the verb *to be* for these situations:

I am 25 years old – Tengo 25 (veinticinco) años

I am scared! – ¡Tengo miedo!

I am very hungry – Tengo mucha hambre

This is the present tense conjugation of the verb *tener*:

I have – yo tengo

You have – tú tienes / usted tiene / vos tenés

He has – él tiene

She has – ella tiene

We have – nosotros tenemos / nosotras tenemos

You have – vosotros tenéis / vosotras tenéis / ustedes tienen

They have – ellos tienen / ellas tienen

After James leaves for the beach and Alex goes to the market, Alicia and María meet Andrea at the hotel's reception:

*ANDREA: Hello, beautiful girls! Are you hungry? – ¡Hola, guapas! ¿**Tenéis** hambre?*

*MARÍA: Yes, I am very hungry – Sí, **tengo** mucha hambre*

*ALICIA: Me too, but I do not have much money – Yo también, pero **tengo** poco dinero*

*ANDREA: It is not a problem. We do not have to go somewhere expensive – No es problema. No **tenemos** que ir a un sitio caro*

*MARÍA: We can go to the restaurant on the corner; I have a friend who works there – Podemos ir al restaurante de la esquina, **tengo** un amigo que trabaja allí*

Lesson 9

Yes, No, Please, Thanks: Basic Vocabulary

Along with the basic verbs you learned in the last lesson, these are also some basic words you need to know to get by: *yes, no, please, thanks*.

yes – sí

no – no

please – por favor

thanks – gracias

Now that you know how to say these four words, you can travel in a Spanish-speaking country without being considered rude.

Let's see a few other expressions and words that might turn out useful in case you want to make a really good impression:

sorry – perdón

I am sorry – lo siento / lo lamento

excuse me – disculpe

thanks – gracias

thank you very much – muchas gracias

you are welcome – de nada

never mind – no hay por qué

it is fine – está bien

of course – claro

of course not – claro que no

absolutely – absolutamente

not at all – para nada

for sure – por supuesto

Let's use all of these in sentences:

*Yes, I also need a ticket – **Sí**, yo también necesito un billete*

*No, I don't eat meat – **No**, no como carne*

*Please, could you point me to the train station? – **Por favor**, ¿podría indicarme dónde está la estación de trenes?*

*Thanks, you are very kind – **Gracias**, eres muy amable*

*Sorry, I did not see you there – **Perdón**, no te vi ahí*

*I am sorry, I do not have any cash on me – **Lo lamento**, no tengo nada de efectivo*

*Excuse me, do you work here? – **Disculpe**, ¿usted trabaja aquí?*

*Thanks, but that is not necessary – **Gracias**, pero eso no es necesario*

*Thank you very much! It is delicious! – **¡Muchas gracias!** ¡Está delicioso!*

*You are welcome, I also have extra water just in case – **De nada**, también tengo agua de más por si acaso*

Never mind, you would have done it for me too – **No hay por qué**, *tú también lo habrías hecho por mí*

It is fine; I do not need anything – **Está bien**; *no necesito nada*

Of course I want to go – **Claro** *que quiero ir*

Of course not, that was not me – **Claro que no**, *ese no fui yo*

Absolutely, I will be there at 7 – **Absolutamente**, *voy a estar ahí a las 7*

Not at all, it was not trouble for me – **Para nada**, *no fue ningún problema*

For sure, tell me what you need, and I will bring it – **Por supuesto**, *dime qué necesitas, y yo te lo traigo*

When James gets back from the beach, he sees Andrea at the hostel reception:

JAMES: Excuse me, Andrea, may I ask you a question? – *Disculpa, Andrea, ¿puedo hacerte una pregunta?*

ANDREA: Of course, James! Whatever you need – *¡Claro, James! Lo que necesites*

JAMES: Thank you – *Gracias*

ANDREA: Don't worry, tell me – *No hay de qué, dime*

JAMES: I am really sorry, but I lost my map – *Lo siento mucho, pero he perdido mi mapa*

ANDREA: Don't worry! We have millions – *¡No te preocupes! Tenemos millones*

JAMES: Are you sure? – *¿Estás segura?*

ANDREA: For sure, yes. Here, take one – *Por supuesto, sí. Aquí, toma uno*

JAMES: Thanks a lot, Andrea, you are the best! – *Muchas gracias, Andrea, ¡eres la mejor!*

ANDREA: Yes, I know! – Sí, ¡lo sé!

Lesson 10

What's Happening? The Present Tense (Part I)

This is not meant to be a boring grammar book, so you won't be driven crazy with conjugation rules that you need to learn by heart. However, what will be explained in this lesson might actually turn to be quite useful to understand why verbs are conjugated the way they are. There is no need to memorize this, but it will inevitably happen once you start learning more and more verbs.

Some of the verbs before were irregular verbs. This means they don't follow the normal rules of conjugation. This is why a verb like *ser* (*to be*) can be conjugated into words that sound nothing like *ser*: *eres* (*you are*), for example—it is completely irregular. Now, luckily for you, most verbs in Spanish are actually *regular*. This means they follow three basic models of conjugation, depending on whether they end on *-ar, -er* or *-ir*.

Regular verbs that end in *-ar* always follow the same structure and add the same letters after the 'root' of the verb. You can find the root of a verb easily. Just take *-ar, -er* or *-ir* off it in its infinitive form and you will have the root. For verb *amar* (*to love*), for example, the root is *am-*.

Amar (*to love*)

yo am**o**

tú am**as** / vos am**ás** / usted am**a**

él/ella am**a**

nosotros am**amos**

ustedes am**an** / vosotros am**áis**

ellos/ellas am**an**

Regular verbs that end in *-er* also follow the same structure and add the same letters after the root of the verb, as in the following example. For the verb *temer* (*to fear*), the root is *tem-*.

Temer (*to fear*)

yo tem**o**

tú tem**es** / vos tem**és** / usted tem**e**

él/ella tem**e**

nosotros tem**emos**

ustedes tem**en** / vosotros tem**éis**

ellos/ellas tem**en**

Regular verbs that end in *-ir* also follow the same structure and add the same letters after the root of the verb, as in the following example. For the verb *vivir* (*to live*), the root is *viv-*.

Vivir (*to live*)

yo viv**o**

tú viv**es** / vos viv**ís** / usted viv**e**

él/ella viv**e**

nosotros viv**imos**

ustedes viv**en** / vosotros viv**ís**

ellos/ellas viv**en**

As you can see, in all cases, for the singular first person, *yo*, you just need to add an *o* to the root of the verb:

*Caminar (to walk): I walk in the park – Yo **camino** en el parque*

*Beber (to drink): I only drink beer – Solo **bebo** cerveza*

*Partir (to leave): I leave tomorrow morning – Yo **parto** mañana por la mañana*

For *tú*, you just add -*as* or -*es*:

*Extrañar (to miss): Do you miss your sister? – ¿**Extrañas** a tu hermana?*

*Creer (to believe): You do not believe in magic – No **crees** en la magia*

*Abrir (to open): Do you open the door? – ¿**Abres** la puerta?*

For *él* or *ella*, you, as in English, normally add an *s*. In Spanish, you just have to add an *a* or *e*:

*Escribir (to write): She never writes – Nunca **escribe***

*Hablar (to talk): He talks too much – Él **habla** demasiado*

*Vender (to sell): She sells her soul for a snack – **Vende** su alma por un bocadillo*

For *nosotros*, you add either -*amos*, -*emos* or -*imos*:

*Alquilar (to rent): We rent the same apartment every year – Todos los años **alquilamos** el mismo piso*

*Aprender (to learn): We never learn! – ¡Nunca **aprendemos**!*

*Asistir (to attend): Tonight we attend the party no matter what – Hoy **asistimos** a la fiesta de cualquier forma*

For *vosotros*, you have to add -*áis*, -*éis* or -*ís*:

*Ayudar (to help): Why don't you help with the cleaning? – ¿Por qué no **ayudáis** con la limpieza?*

*Leer (to read): You read all day – **Leéis** todo el día*

*Compartir (to share): You share everything you do on social media – **Compartís** todo lo que hacéis en redes sociales*

Finally, for *ellos, ellas,* and *ustedes*, you have to add *-an* or *-en* to the root of the verb:

*Cocinar (to cook): They cook every night – **Cocinan** todas las noches*

*Responder (to answer): You always answer late – Ustedes siempre **responden** tarde*

*Decidir (to decide): They decide what to do with their lives – Ellas **deciden** qué hacer con sus vidas*

James and Alex want to surprise the girls. They are cooking dinner for everybody! They are in the hostel's kitchen making some risotto with vegetables and seafood:

*ALEX: How lucky you are here! I cook very bad – ¡Qué suerte que estás aquí! Yo **cocino** muy mal*

*JAMES: Do you think I am a chef, or something like that? I'm not so good – ¿**Crees** que soy un chef o algo así? No soy tan bueno*

*ALEX: We help each other – Nos **ayudamos** el uno al otro*

*JAMES: I learn a few things about rice while we do this – **Aprendo** algunas cosas sobre el arroz mientras lo hacemos*

*ALEX: Like what? – ¿Qué **aprendes**?*

*JAMES: That it gets done faster while I drink beer – Que se **cocina** más rápido cuando **bebo** cerveza*

*ALEX: I miss Australian beer! – ¡**Extraño** la cerveza australiana!*

*JAMES: There is a bar nearby where they sell Foster's – Hay un bar cerca de aquí donde **venden** Foster's*

*ALEX: Really? I'm leaving right now – ¿De veras? **Parto** ahora mismo*

*JAMES: No way! You help me until we are done and after dinner I will take you there – ¡De ningún modo! Me **ayudas** hasta que terminemos y después de cenar te llevo.*

Lesson 11

What's Happening?: The Present Tense (Part II)

There is another way to talk about things that *are actually happening* right now.

The construction of the present conjugation of verb *estar* + the gerund of another verb is very similar to the English present continuous: *I am cooking, I am talking, I am walking.*

While the English gerund always ends with *-ing*, the Spanish gerund ends in *-ando* or *-endo*.

Cocinar (To cook)

yo **estoy** cocin**ando**

tú **estás** cocin**ando** / vos **estás** cocin**ando** / usted **está** cocin**ando**

él/ella **está** cocin**ando**

nosotros **estamos** cocin**ando**

ustedes **están** cocin**ando** / vosotros **estáis** cocin**ando** ellos/ellas **están** cocin**ando**

Beber (to drink)

yo **estoy** beb**iendo**

tú **estás** beb**iendo** / vos **estás** beb**iendo** / usted **está** beb**iendo**

él/ella **está** beb**iendo**

nosotros **estamos** beb**iendo**

ustedes **están** beb**iendo** / vosotros **estáis** beb**iendo**

ellos/ellas **están** beb**iendo**

Escribir (to write)

yo **estoy** escrib**iendo**

tú **estás** escrib**iendo** / vos **estás** escrib**iendo** / usted **está** escrib**iendo**

él/ella **está** escrib**iendo**

nosotros **estamos** escrib**iendo**

ustedes **están** escrib**iendo** / vosotros **estáis** escrib**iendo**

ellos/ellas **están** escrib**iendo**

These are some sentences with verb *estar* + gerund that you might use a lot while traveling:

I am traveling – Estoy viajando

I am getting to know Spain – Estoy conociendo España

I am learning Spanish – Estoy aprendiendo español

I am taking a year off – Me estoy tomando un año sabático

I am falling in love with this country – Me estoy enamorando de este país

You might use this construction a lot while making plans:

I am leaving – Me estoy yendo (yendo is the gerund of verb ir, to go)

I am going to your hotel – Estoy yendo a tu hotel

I am coming – Estoy yendo

Juan is calling a taxi – Juan está llamando un taxi

The food is arriving – La comida está llegando

You can definitely use *estar* + gerund to talk about your life at present:

I am working for a company – Estoy trabajando en una empresa

I am studying in university – Estoy estudiando en la universidad

I am saving money to travel some more – Estoy ahorrando para viajar más

I am thinking about quitting my job – Estoy pensando en renunciar

James and Alex's meal is ready, but the girls are nowhere to be seen:

JAMES: Do you think they are coming? – ¿Crees que **están viniendo***?*

ALEX: I don't know. I'm texting María – No lo sé. **Estoy escribiendo** *un mensaje a María*

MARÍA: Who are you texting? – ¿A quién **estás escribiendo***?*

JAMES: Girls! You are here! – ¡Chicas! ¡Estáis aquí!

ANDREA: Yes, and we are starving – Sí, nos **estamos muriendo** *de hambre*

ALEX: That is great because we are waiting for you with a surprise – Eso es genial, porque las **estamos esperando** *con una sorpresa*

ALICIA: Is that a risotto or am I hallucinating? – ¿Eso es un risotto o **estoy alucinando***?*

ALEX AND JAMES: Surprise!!! – ¡¡¡Sorpresa!!!

Here are some other examples of this construction:

Verb *to buy – comprar: I am buying a surfboard –* **Estoy comprando** *una tabla de surf*

Verb *to travel – viajar: You are traveling a lot – **Estás viajando** mucho*

Verb *to book – reservar: We are booking a room – **Estamos reservando** una habitación*

Verb *to talk – hablar: They are talking – Ellos **están hablando***

Lesson 12

Do I Know You?: Useful Verbs When Meeting People (Part I)

Meeting people is not just saying *hello* and *how are you?* If you do not want your conversations in Spanish to end after one or two sentences, you will need a few more tools to know about yourself and others.

James is not only traveling around South America; he is also taking Spanish lessons everywhere he goes. In Cartagena, he has booked private classes at a local university.

He gets there at ten a.m. and meets professor González, who is going to be his tutor for a couple of weeks.

As for pronouns, since only two people are interacting, you will find the pronoun *I* (*yo*) and the formal and informal versions of *you* (*tú* and *usted*). As you will see, James will use the formal version of *you*, *usted*, to address the professor. The professor, on the other hand, uses informal *tú* to speak to him.

As for verbs, you will find some of the verbs explained earlier: *ser*, *estar*, and *tener*. There are other verbs as well: *conocer*, *encontrarse*, *comenzar*, *desear*, *saber*, and *querer*. These verbs will be explained in detail later.

PROF. GONZÁLEZ: Hello, it is nice to meet you. How are you? – Hola, es un placer <u>conocerte</u>. ¿Cómo <u>te encuentras</u>?

JAMES: Good morning, professor. The pleasure is mine. I am doing very well, and you? – Buenos días, profesor. El placer es mío. Me encuentro muy bien, ¿y usted?

PROF. GONZÁLEZ: I am very well! Talk to me about yourself before we start – ¡Estoy muy bien! Dime algo sobre ti antes de <u>comenzar</u>

JAMES: Of course! What do you wish to know? – ¡Por supuesto! ¿Qué <u>desea</u> <u>saber</u>?

PROF. GONZÁLEZ: I already know your name, but I want to know your age and your occupation – Ya <u>sé</u> tu nombre, pero <u>quiero</u> <u>saber</u> tu edad y tu ocupación

JAMES: Sure. I am 25 years old, and I am a journalist – Claro. Tengo 25 años, y soy periodista

PROF. GONZÁLEZ: Oh, that is very interesting. What kind of a journalist? – Oh, eso es muy interesante. ¿Qué tipo de periodista?

JAMES: I want to be a travel writer – <u>Quiero</u> ser un escritor de viajes

PROF. GONZÁLEZ: Is that why you want to know Spanish? – ¿Por eso <u>quieres</u> <u>saber</u> español?

JAMES: Yes, exactly! – Sí, ¡exacto!

With this in mind, the underlined verbs you found in the previous conversation will be explained in detail: *conocer*, *saber*, *encontrar*, *encontrarse*, *decir*, *comenzar*, *empezar*, *desear*, and *querer*.

These verbs are quite common and can be really useful when you get to know a new person.

You will be shown the basic conjugations in the present tense and given some practical examples for each of them so you can engage in conversation and sound like a real pro in Spanish.

Conocer and *saber*

Conocer and *saber* both mean *to know*, but they are not synonyms.

Conocer is used to talk about familiarity with people and places. Let's see the conjugation for the present tense of the verb *conocer* and some examples:

I know – yo conozco

You know – tú conoces / usted conoce / vos conocés

He knows – él conoce

She knows – ella conoce

We know – nosotros conocemos / nosotras conocemos

You know – vosotros conocéis / vosotras conocéis / ustedes conocen

They know – ellos conocen / ellas conocen

Here are some real-life examples with the verb *conocer*:

*I know a good restaurant around here – **Conozco** un buen restaurante por esta zona*

*Do you know María – ¿**Conoces** a María?*

*Sara knows England – Sara **conoce** Inglaterra*

*We know the best hostel in this city – **Conocemos** el mejor hostal de esta ciudad*

*Do you know Colombian singer Carlos Vives? – ¿**Conocéis** al cantante Colombiano Carlos Vives?*

*Do they know the museum? – ¿Ellas **conocen** el museo?*

What about this phrase?

It is a pleasure to meet you – Es un placer conocerte

In this case, just like in English, the verb is not conjugated, but it is in its infinitive form: *conocer*. The little particle *-te* means *you*, as in *meet you*.

As mentioned, *conocer* is used for understanding of people and places: *conocer a alguien* (*to know someone*) and *conocer un lugar* (*to know a place*). The verb *saber*, the other *to know* verb, is used to express knowledge of facts or the possession of skills.

Let's look at the verb's conjugation and some practical examples:

I know – yo sé

You know – tú sabes / usted sabe / vos sabés

He knows – él sabe

She knows – ella sabe

We know – nosotros sabemos / nosotras sabemos

You know – vosotros sabéis / vosotras sabéis / ustedes saben

They know – ellos saben / ellas saben

I know how to add numbers! – ¡Sé sumar!

Do you know how to speak Spanish? – ¿Sabes hablar español?

Do you know what is my train's platform? – ¿Sabe cuál es el andén de mi tren?

We know lots of things about this place – Sabemos muchas cosas sobre este lugar

They know how to throw a party – Ellas saben cómo organizar una fiesta

Now, to really understand the difference, let's see some combined examples with both *conocer* and *saber*:

I know the museum and I know perfectly well where it is – Conozco el museo y sé perfectamente dónde está

*Ana does not know Juan, but she knows who he is – Ana no **conoce** a Juan, pero **sabe** quién es*

*You and me know each other very well; we know what we are thinking – Tú y yo nos **conocemos** muy bien, **sabemos** lo que piensa el otro*

Back at the hostel in Cartagena, James is asking for directions to go to San Andrés island to his friends.

*JAMES: Guys, do you know San Andrés island? – Chicos, ¿**conocéis** la isla de San Andrés?*

*MARÍA: Of course! It is beautiful. You do not know it? – ¡Por supuesto! Es hermosa. ¿No la **conoces**?*

*JAMES: Not yet, but I want to know it. Do you know the best way to get there? – No aún, pero quiero conocerla. ¿**Sabéis** cuál es la mejor forma de llegar?*

*ALEX: I know a shortcut! You go to the beach… and you swim straight! – ¡Yo **conozco** un atajo! Vas a la playa… ¡y nadas todo recto!*

JAMES: Very funny, Alex – Muy gracioso, Alex

*MARÍA: The best way is to fly… unless you know someone with a boat – La mejor forma es volar… a menos que **conozcas** a alguien que tenga un barco*

*JAMES: Who knows? Maybe someday… – ¿Quién **sabe**? Quizá algún día…*

Lesson 13

Do I know You?: Useful Verbs When Meeting People (Part II)

In the last lesson, you learned some common verbs that are quite useful when you are getting to know people. Now, you are going to see some more of them:

Encontrar **and** *encontrarse*

Encontrar is quite a common verb, and it means *to find*. You will not find this verb as useful as its *pronominal* form, *encontrarse*, while meeting people. Let's see the simple form first so that you can understand the difference between the two.

This is the present tense conjugation of the verb *encontrar*:

I find – yo encuentro

You find – tú encuentras / usted encuentra / vos encontrás

He finds – él encuentra

She finds – ella encuentra

We find – nosotros encontramos

You find – vosotros encontráis / ustedes encuentran

They find – ellos encuentran / ellas encuentran

Let's see how to use this verb in some examples:

*I cannot find my camera! – ¡No **encuentro** mi cámara de fotos!*

*James always has trouble to find his pen – James nunca **encuentra** su bolígrafo*

*Laura cannot find a place in a hostel; it is all booked! – Laura no **encuentra** lugar en un hostal; ¡está todo reservado!*

*Every day we find a new restaurant we like – Todos los días **encontramos** un nuevo restaurante que nos gusta*

Now, as mentioned before, there is another version of this verb that has the particle *-se* at the end: *encontrarse.*

All verbs ending in *-se* are called *pronominal* verbs.

There is no need to remember that word; you just need to know that these verbs require a little word (*me, te, se, nos, os, se*) next to the conjugated verb. The little word depends on the pronoun (*yo, tú, él, nosotros,* etc.). It is placed before the conjugated verb (when it is placed afterward, then it is an order! But let's not get into that yet).

Encontrarse means *to be, to feel* or *to meet.* Yes, it has three meanings, hence why it is useful for you to learn it, especially if you want to meet (and *meet with*) people: you can use it when you are asking people how they feel and when you are making plans.

Let's see how to conjugate it first, and then some real-life examples are provided:

Yo me encuentro

Tú te encuentras / usted se encuentra / vos te encontrás

Él se encuentra

Ella se encuentra

Nosotros nos encontramos

Vosotros os encontráis / ustedes se encuentran

Ellos se encuentran / ellas se encuentran

Here are some examples for this particular verb:

*I am okay – Yo **me encuentro** bien*

*Tomorrow I meet with Sara at a coffee shop – Mañana **me encuentro** con Sara en un café*

*She feels tired – Ella **se encuentra** cansada*

*Pablo is not feeling very well – Pablo no **se encuentra** muy bien*

*We meet at the train station in ten minutes – **Nos encontramos** en la estación de tren en diez minutos*

Some other pronominal verbs and examples:

*To get married – casarse (I get married in October – **Me caso** en octubre)*

*To get dressed – vestirse (Juan already gets dressed on his own – Juan ya **se viste** solo)*

*To look – verse (Do we look fine? – ¿**Nos vemos** bien?)*

*To get – ponerse (The kids get really cranky at this time – Los niños **se ponen** muy fastidiosos a esta hora)*

*To sit down – sentarse (Do we sit down? – ¿**Nos sentamos**?)*

James made plans to meet with Alex and María at the beach. They are talking on the phone because they cannot find each other:

JAMES: Hi, María, can you hear me? – Hola, María, ¿me oyes?

*MARÍA: Yes, I hear you, are you okay? – Sí, te oigo. ¿**te encuentras** bien?*

*JAMES: I am doing great! – ¡**Me encuentro** muy bien!*

*MARÍA: Great! Are we meeting at the beach? – ¡Genial! ¿**Nos encontramos** en la playa?*

JAMES: *Sure, I am already here, at the beach* – *Claro, ya **me encuentro** aquí, en la playa*

MARÍA: *We are also at the beach* – *¡Nosotros también **nos encontramos** en la playa!*

JAMES: *I cannot see you, can you see me?* – *No os veo, ¿vosotros me veis?*

MARÍA: *Are you near the sea? Can you raise an arm?* – *¿**Te encuentras** cerca del mar? ¿Puedes alzar un brazo?*

JAMES: *Sure* – *Claro*

MARÍA: *I see you!* – *¡Te veo!*

Comenzar and *empezar*

Comenzar means *to start*. There is another Spanish verb that means the same, *empezar*. Let's see the conjugation in the present tense and some examples you might find useful:

I start – *yo comienzo*

You start – *tú comienzas* / *usted comienza* / *vos comenzás*

He starts – *él comienza*

She starts – *ella comienza*

We start – *nosotros comenzamos* / *nosotras comenzamos*

You start – *vosotros comenzáis* / *vosotras comenzáis* / *ustedes comienzan*

They start – *ellos comienzan* / *ellas comienzan*

I start – *yo empiezo*

You start – *tú empiezas* / *usted empieza* / *vos empezás*

He starts – *él empieza*

She starts – *ella empieza*

We start – *nosotros empezamos* / *nosotras empezamos*

You start – vosotros empezáis / vosotras empezáis / ustedes empiezan

They start – ellos empiezan / ellas empiezan

These two verbs are synonyms, so you can choose the one you like the most or the one that is most widely used in the country you are visiting. Normally, in Spain, they use *empezar,* and in most of Latin America they prefer *comenzar*, but any Spanish-speaking person will understand either without any inconvenience:

I start my trip in Colombia – **Comienzo** *mi viaje en Colombia /* **Empiezo** *mi viaje en Colombia*

Lucía starts studying again in two weeks – Lucía **comienza** *a estudiar de nuevo en dos semanas / Lucía* **empieza** *a estudiar de nuevo en dos semanas*

We start cooking now! – ¡Ya **comenzamos** *a cocinar! / ¡Ya* **empezamos** *a cocinar!*

James, back at the hostel, is talking with one of the Mexican girls, Daniela, about their trips:

JAMES: Dani, is your trip starting or finishing? – Dani, ¿tu viaje está **empezando** *o terminando?*

DANIELA: My trip has just started! Me and my friends are going down to the south of Argentina, and then we start going up to Ecuador – ¡Mi viaje recién **comienza**! *Yo y mis amigas bajamos hasta Argentina, y luego* **empezamos** *a subir a Ecuador*

JAMES: For how long are you traveling? –– ¿Por cuánto tiempo viajan?

DANIELA: We start with a one-month plan... But I think the trip is starting to grow – **Comenzamos** *con un plan de un mes... pero creo que el viaje* **empieza** *a extenderse*

JAMES: You do not need to go back to Mexico to start your classes? – ¿No debes volver a México para **comenzar** *con tus clases?*

*DANIELA: Oh, no! I already graduated. When I come back, I have to start working – ¡Oh, no! Ya me he graduado. Cuando vuelva, debo **empezar** a trabajar*

Desear and *querer*

Two verbs in Spanish can be translated as *to want*. In some situations, you can use either of them, but they are not real synonyms. *Querer* can express *to want*, *to care,* and *to love*, while *desear* can express *to want*, *to desire,* and *to wish*.

You do not need to remember this by heart. The conjugations for these two verbs are presented later and, afterward, some examples so you can learn their meanings with practice.

I want – yo deseo

You want – tú deseas / usted desea / vos deseás

He wants – él desea

She wants – ella desea

We want – nosotros deseamos / nosotras deseamos

You want – vosotros deseáis / vosotras deseáis / ustedes desean

They want – ellos desean / ellas desean

I want – yo quiero

You want – tú quieres / usted quiere / vos querés

He wants – él quiere

She wants – ella quiere

We want – nosotros queremos / nosotras queremos

You want – vosotros queréis / vosotras queréis / ustedes quieren

They want – ellos quieren / ellas quieren

Let's see some examples of situations you could use each verb:

*I want to meet your brother – **Quiero/deseo** conocer a tu hermano*

*I wish you good luck – Te **deseo** buena suerte*

*Do you love me? – ¿Me **quieres**?*

James is making plans with Daniela to go out together:

*JAMES: Do you want to grab a coffee afterward? – ¿**Quieres** ir a tomar un café más tarde?*

*DANIELA: No! I mean... yes, I want to go out with you, but I do not want to drink coffee; I do not like coffee – ¡No! **Quiero** decir... sí, **deseo** salir contigo, pero no **quiero** beber café; no me gusta el café*

*JAMES: Do you want to have a drink tonight, then? – ¿**Deseas** ir a beber un trago a la noche, entonces?*

*DANELA: Sure, at what time do you want to go? –- Claro, ¿a qué hora **quieres** ir?*

*JAMES: At eight, is that good? There is a bar around the corner I want to try – A las ocho, ¿te parece bien? Hay un bar a la vuelta que **deseo** probar*

Lesson 14

Come Again?: Understanding Each Other

No matter how hard you study, there are some situations in which communication is not fluent. Maybe the person you are talking to has a really strong accent, or they are speaking very fast. For those situations, you need to be prepared as well!

Here are some practical sentences you might find useful when you get lost in translation:

I do not understand – No <u>comprendo</u> / No <u>entiendo</u>

Please speak slowly – Por favor, <u>hable</u> despacio

Can you say that again, please? – ¿Podría <u>decir</u> eso nuevamente, por favor?

Do you speak English? (formal) – *¿<u>Habla</u> inglés?*

Do you speak Spanish? (formal) – *¿<u>Habla</u> español?*

Do you speak English? (informal) – *¿<u>Hablas</u> inglés?*

Do you speak Spanish? (informal) – *¿<u>Hablas</u> español?*

Can I ask you something? – *¿Puedo <u>preguntarle</u> algo?*

What is the meaning of this? – *¿Qué <u>significa</u> esto?*

In these sentences, there are some basic verbs you need to know when you are trying to be understood by Spanish-speaking people: *hablar, decir, comprender, entender, significar,* and *preguntar*.

Let's see them one by one—what they mean and how you can use them in different situations.

Hablar

Hablar is a very important verb when you are learning a new language. Do not forget the *h* is mute. You will use it a lot in its infinitive form to talk about your ability to speak Spanish. For those situations, you can use some of these sentences:

I am learning to speak Spanish – *Estoy aprendiendo a **hablar** en español*

I do not know how to speak Spanish yet! – *No sé **hablar** español ¡todavía!*

I know how to speak Spanish, but not very well – *Sé **hablar** español, pero no muy bien*

Do you speak English? (informal) – *¿Sabes **hablar** en inglés?*

This is the conjugation for the present tense of the verb *hablar*:

I talk – yo hablo

You talk – tú hablas / usted habla / vos hablás

He talks – él habla

She talks – ella habla

We talk – nosotros hablamos / nosotras hablamos

You talk – vosotros habláis / vosotras habláis / ustedes hablan

They talk – ellos hablan / ellas hablan

Here are some practical examples with the different conjugations:

*I speak Spanish – **Hablo** español*

*I do not speak Spanish – No **hablo** español*

*I speak four languages… more or less – **Hablo** cuatro idiomas… más o menos*

*You speak very fast! Slow down, please – ¡**Hablas** muy rápido! Más despacio, por favor*

*She speaks very well because she practices continuously – Ella **habla** muy bien porque practica continuamente*

*Do you speak English? (formal) – ¿**Habla** usted inglés?*

*He does not know what he is talking about – No sabe de qué **habla***

*Shall we speak Spanish? – ¿**Hablamos** en español?*

*Sometimes we speak in English, sometimes we speak in Spanish – A veces **hablamos** en inglés, a veces **hablamos** en español*

James is out on a date with Dani, the Mexican girl he met at the hostel. They are talking… about talking:

*DANI: Am I talking too fast? You can tell me – ¿Estoy **hablando** demasiado rápido? Puedes decirme*

*JAMES: No, you do not speak fast… Well, you do speak fast, but you speak very clearly – No, no **hablas** rápido… Bueno, sí **hablas** rápido, pero **hablas** muy claramente*

DANI: Good, I stay at ease – Bien, me quedo tranquila

*JAMES: Your friend Sara does speak too fast – Tu amiga Sara sí **habla** muy rápido*

*DANI: I know! Even I have a hard time to understand her when she talks – ¡Lo sé! Incluso yo tengo problemas para comprender cuando **habla***

Decir and *significar*

Decir means *to say*. When communicating with people in Spanish, especially at first, there can be many situations in which you can find this verb useful. Let's see the present tense conjugation for the verb *decir*, then some real-life examples:

I say – yo digo

You say – tú dices / usted dice / vos decís

He says – él dice

She says – ella dice

We say – nosotros decimos / nosotras decimos

You say – vosotros decís / vosotras decís / ustedes dicen

They say – ellos dicen / ellas dicen

Decir can also be used together with the verb *querer* (*to want*). When these two verbs are put together, they get a new meaning:

*'Croqueta' is a funny word; what does it mean? – 'Croqueta es una palabra graciosa; ¿qué **quiere decir**?*

*I like your tattoo. What does it mean? – Me gusta tu tatuaje. ¿Qué **quiere decir**?*

*I do not understand those signs; what do they mean? – No comprendo esos letreros; ¿qué **quieren decir**?*

There is another verb in Spanish that can be used in the same way, to express meaning: *significar*. Let's see the same examples with this verb:

*'Croqueta' is a funny word; what does it mean? – 'Croqueta es una palabra graciosa; ¿qué **significa**?*

*I like your tattoo. What does it mean? – Me gusta tu tatuaje. ¿Qué **significa**?*

*I do not understand those signs; what do they mean? – No comprendo esos letreros; ¿qué **significan**?*

Comprender / Entender

This is one of the first things any traveler has to learn: how to say *I do not understand*!

The two Spanish verbs *entender* and *comprender* are synonyms; they both mean *to understand*. Let's see their present tense conjugation, then some real-life examples, so you know how to apply them:

I understand – yo comprendo

You understand – tú comprendes / usted comprende / vos comprendés

He understands – él comprende

She understands – ella comprende

We understand – nosotros comprendemos / nosotras comprendemos

You understand – vosotros comprendéis / vosotras comprendéis / ustedes comprenden

They understand – ellos comprenden / ellas comprenden

I understand – yo entiendo

You understand – tú entiendes / usted entiende / vos entendés

He understands – él entiende

She understands – ella entiende

We understand – nosotros entendemos / nosotras entendemos

You understand – vosotros entendéis / vosotras entendéis / ustedes entienden

They understand – ellos entienden / ellas entienden

Here are some practical sentences with the verb *comprender*:

*I understand – **Comprendo***

*I do not understand – No **comprendo***

*Do you understand what I say? – ¿**Comprendes** lo que digo?*

We understand almost everything, if you speak slowly – **Comprendemos** *casi todo, si habla lentamente*

She understands Spanish very well, but she finds it hard to speak it – **Comprende** *muy bien el español, pero le cuesta hablarlo*

There are some accents that are hard to understand – Hay algunos acentos difíciles de **comprender**

I do not understand what you are saying – No **comprendo** *lo que dices*

I do not understand what this is – No **comprendo** *qué es esto*

I do not understand what you want to do – No **comprendo** *qué quieres hacer*

I do not understand where you want to go – No **comprendo** *a dónde quieres ir*

Here are the same examples with the verb *entender*:

I understand – **Entiendo**

I do not understand – No **entiendo**

*Do you understand what I say? – ¿***Entiendes** *lo que digo?*

We understand almost everything, if you speak slowly – **Entendemos** *casi todo, si habla lentamente*

She understands Spanish very well, but she finds it hard to speak it – **Entiende** *muy bien el español, pero le cuesta hablarlo*

There are some accents that are hard to understand – Hay algunos acentos difíciles de **entender**

I do not understand what you are saying – No **entiendo** *lo que dices*

I do not understand what this is – No **entiendo** *qué es esto*

I do not understand what you want to do – No **entiendo** *qué quieres hacer*

*I do not understand where you want to go – No **entiendo** a dónde quieres ir*

Preguntar

Preguntar means *to ask*. Never be afraid to ask questions. Most people will be glad to answer them. To ask questions in Spanish, the first thing you should learn is how to ask:

May I ask you something? (formal) – *¿Puedo hacerle una pregunta?*

Can I ask you a question? (informal) – *¿Puedo preguntarte algo?*

Sorry, I have a question… – Perdón, una pregunta…

This is the present tense conjugation for the verb *preguntar*:

I ask – yo pregunto

You ask – tú preguntas / usted pregunta / vos preguntás

He asks – él pregunta

She asks – ella pregunta

We ask – nosotros preguntamos / nosotras preguntamos

You ask – vosotros preguntáis / vosotras preguntáis / ustedes preguntan

They ask – ellos preguntan / ellas preguntan

James and Dani are hanging out in the common room. After their date the night before, they have spent most of their time together:

JAMES: Dani, may I ask you something? – Dani, ¿puedo preguntarte algo?

DANI: Of course! Ask me whatever you want – ¡Claro! Pregúntame lo que quieras

JAMES: Is there someone special in your life? – ¿Hay alguien especial en tu vida?

DANI: Well, yes. Many people: my mom, my dad, my grandma – Pues, sí. Mucha gente: mi mamá, mi papá, mi abuela…

JAMES: Haha, no, that's not what I am asking – Jaja, no, eso no es lo que estoy preguntando

DANI: What are you asking then? –- ¿Qué me preguntas, entonces?

JAMES: I was wondering if you have a partner – Me preguntaba si tienes pareja

DANI: Oh, that is what you are asking! – Oh, ¡eso es lo que preguntas!

JAMES: What is your answer? – ¿Cuál es tu respuesta?

DANI: No, I do not have a boyfriend, that is my answer – No, no tengo novio, esa es mi respuesta

Vocabulary for going out

¿Puedo comprarte algo de beber? – May I buy you something to drink?

¿Vienes aquí a menudo? – Do you come here often?

¿De qué trabajas? – So, what do you do for a living?

¿Quieres bailar? – Do you want to dance?

¿Quieres tomar aire fresco? – Would you like to get some fresh air?

¿Quieres ir a otra fiesta? – Do you want to go to a different party?

¡Vayámonos de aquí! – Let's get out of here!

¿Mi casa o tu casa? – My place or yours?

¿Quieres ver una película en mi casa? – Would you like to watch a movie at my place?

¿Tienes planes para esta noche? – Do you have any plans for tonight?

¿Te gustaría comer conmigo uno de estos días? – Would you like to eat with me sometime?

¿Quieres ir a tomar un café? – Would you like to go get a coffee?

¿Puedo acompañarte/llevarte a tu casa? – May I walk/drive you home?

¿Quieres que nos volvamos a ver? – Would you like to meet again?

¡Gracias por una hermosa noche! – Thank you for a lovely evening!

¿Quieres entrar y tomar una taza de café? – Would you like to come inside for a coffee?

¡Eres hermoso/a! – You're gorgeous!

¡Eres gracioso/a! – You're funny!

¡Tienes unos ojos hermosos! – You have beautiful eyes!

¡Bailas muy bien! – You're a great dancer!

¡He estado pensando en ti todo el día! – I have been thinking about you all day!

¡Ha sido muy agradable charlar contigo! – It's been really nice talking to you!

Lesson 15

Goodbye! Let's meet again!

James is leaving Colombia. It is a sad day at the hostel because all of the regulars (María, Alex, Alicia, Andrea, Daniela, and the Mexican girls) grew very fond of him... But he has to move on. He has a flight booked to Lima, Perú.

You can surely learn something from James' departure. For example, how to say *goodbye*.

Bye! – ¡Chau!

Goodbye – Adiós

See you – Nos vemos

See you later – Hasta luego

See you soon – Nos vemos pronto

See you tomorrow – Hasta mañana

It was a pleasure to meet you – Fue un placer conocerte

I hope we meet again – Espero que nos volvamos a ver

Have a nice day – Tenga un buen día

Have a good weekend! – ¡Buen fin de semana!

Take care – Cuídate

Everyone is gathered at the hostel's reception to say goodbye to James:

JAMES: Okay, guys, I really should be leaving now, my plane is leaving in two hours… My taxi is here! – Okay, chicos, realmente debería irme ahora, mi avión sale en dos horas… ¡Mi taxi está aquí!

ALEX: You are not leaving without giving me another hug, mate! – ¡No te vas sin antes darme otro abrazo, amigo!

ANDREA: It was a real pleasure to meet you, James – Fue un verdadero placer conocerte, James

ALICIA: When are you coming back? – ¿Cuándo regresas?

JAMES: Well, I don't know. Soon, I hope – Bueno, no lo sé. Pronto, espero

MARÍA: I wish you the best of luck for the rest of your trip – Te deseo la mejor de las suertes para el resto de tu viaje

JAMES: Thanks to all of you, really. Dani, don't cry! We will see each other someday – Gracias a todos, de verdad. Dani, ¡no llores! Nos veremos algún día

DANI: I know! I know! I am going to miss you – ¡Lo sé! ¡Lo sé! Te voy a extrañar

JAMES: Me too… I'm going to miss you all – Yo también… Los voy a extrañar a todos

ANDREA: Your taxi is getting impatient… – Tu taxi se está poniendo impaciente…

JAMES: All right, bye, guys! We'll see each other soon! Thank you for everything – Bien, ¡chau, chicos! ¡Nos veremos pronto! Gracias por todo

ALL: Goodbye, James! – ¡Adiós, James!

But what about technology? Nowadays, just because you do not see someone physically anymore does not mean you cannot stay in touch with them.

Here are some sentences that might be useful if you want to keep in touch with someone:

Let's keep in touch – Mantengámonos en contacto

Call me – Llámame

What is your phone number? – ¿Cuál es tu número de teléfono?

Write to me – Escríbeme

Follow me on Instagram – Sígueme en Instagram

Can I add you on Facebook so we can keep in touch? – ¿Puedo añadirte a mis amigos en Facebook para que estemos en contacto?

Give me your email address – Dame tu dirección de email

What's your email address? – ¿Cómo es tu dirección de correo electrónico?

Do you use Snapchat? – ¿Tienes Snapchat?

If you have to send an email in Spanish for work, studies, accommodation or any other formal setting, these are some ways you can say hello, introduce yourself, and say goodbye:

Dear, Andrea, – Estimada, Andrea,

My name is James – Mi nombre es James

I am contacting you because... – Le escribo porque...

If it is not an inconvenience to you – Si no supone inconvenientes para usted

Looking forward to hearing from you – Espero su respuesta

Kind regards – Saludos cordiales

James is going to Peru next. When James arrives in Peru, he will not stay in a hostel. He will be 'couchsurfing' instead.

This means he got in touch with another traveler through a specific website earlier, and now the other person is going to let him stay in their house for free!

Before leaving for the airport, James sends Damián, the other traveler, an email to remind him that he is arriving that afternoon:

Estimado, Damián,

Dear, Damián,

¡Espero que estés bien!

I hope you are doing great!

Te escribo para recordarte que hoy es mi vuelo a Perú.

I am writing to remind you I am flying to Peru today.

Estoy saliendo de mi hostal en Cartagena en algunos minutos.

I'm leaving my hostel in Cartagena in a few minutes.

Mi avión sale al mediodía.

My plane is departing at noon.

Llegará a Lima cerca de las tres y media de la tarde.

It will arrive in Lima around half past three in the afternoon.

Voy a tomar un taxi hasta tu casa.

I am taking a taxi to your house.

No tengo ganas de tomar el bus; estoy algo cansado...

I do not feel like taking a bus; I am a little bit tired...

Llevo unas botellas de vino para compartir contigo.

I'm taking some bottles of wine to share with you.

Y más tarde, puedo cocinar.

And later, I can prepare dinner.

Bueno, ¡eso es todo!

Well, that is it!

Mis amigos del hostal me esperan para despedirme.

My friends from the hostel are waiting for me to say goodbye.

Voy a extrañarlos mucho.

I am really going to miss them.

Nos vemos más tarde.

See you later.

¡Chau!

Bye!

Lesson 16

It All Adds Up: Basic Numbers!

Numbers are not just for mathematicians. You need to know numbers if you want to buy something, tell someone your age, ask the time, tell the date, say how many cats you have… and so on.

For now, here are the first ten numbers in Spanish:

1 – uno / un / una

2 – dos

3 – tres

4 – cuatro

5 – cinco

6 – seis

7 – siete

8 – ocho

9 – nueve

10 – diez

Number one!

While *uno* is *number one*, there are also the articles *un* and *una* that are the equivalent of the English indefinite article *a* (or *an*).

When you put the number 1 next to a word, you do not say, for example, *uno coche*, but *un coche*, even if you are emphasizing the quantity of cars you have.

I have a car – Tengo un coche

I have one car – Tengo un coche

However, if you are just counting, you say *uno, dos, tres, cuatro* (*one, two, three, four*). Or, if you are adding numbers, you say *uno más uno es dos* (*one plus one is two*).

Let's take this opportunity to see some examples of sentences with indefinite articles in Spanish. Nouns are randomly male or female. Since there is not many 'male' or 'female' nouns in English, it might be hard, at first, to remember what each word is, but with practice you will remember.

Here are some examples of masculine nouns:

*I want a new phone – Quiero **un teléfono** nuevo*

*Let's play a game! – ¡Juguemos **un juego**!*

*Do you have a pen? – ¿Tienes **un bolígrafo**?*

*There is a road – Hay **un camino***

*I want to buy a notebook – Quiero comprar **un cuaderno***

*Can you recommend a book? – ¿Me recomiendas **un libro**?*

*I have lost a shoe – Perdí **un zapato***

*Shall we drink a coffee? – ¿Tomamos **un café**?*

*I have a problem – Tengo **un problema***

Here are some examples of feminine nouns:

*Bring a chair – Trae **una silla***

*Let's go to a party – Vamos a **una fiesta***

*I need a new table – Necesito **una mesa** nueva*

*It was a hard night – Fue **una noche** difícil*

*I went to a yoga class – Fui a **una clase** de yoga*

*Take a picture – Toma **una foto***

*Give me a hand – Dame **una mano***

What about the plural? Wait! How come a word that means *one* can have a plural? In English, you would say *some* or *a few*, but in Spanish, you say *unos* or *unas*.

Here are some examples:

*I saw him a few days ago – Lo vi hace **unos días***

*I brought you some apples – Te traje **unas manzanas***

*There are some really nice beaches here – Hay **unas playas** muy lindas aquí*

*Some men visited her – **Unos hombres** la visitaron*

How Many?: Quantities

Let's use the first ten numbers to learn some practical examples with small amounts. The numbers are written both with cyphers and words.

*I have two children – Tengo **dos** (2) hijos*

*There are three free rooms in this hotel – Hay **tres** (3) habitaciones libres en este hotel*

*Let's order four more beers – Pidamos **cuatro** (4) cervezas más*

*I'm traveling with my five best friends – Estoy viajando con mis **cinco** (5) mejores amigos*

*Give me six oranges, please – Deme **seis** (6) naranjas, por favor*

*Your mother has called seven times – Tu madre ha llamado **siete** (7) veces*

*My brother has eight cats – Mi hermano tiene **ocho** (8) gatos*

*I want to make a reservation for nine nights – Quiero hacer una reserva por **nueve** (9) noches*

James is going to be couchsurfing at Damián's house. Damián is a young Peruvian architect and loves traveling. He has also stayed in other people's houses for free while traveling, so now he wants to return the favor. Also, this is how he gets to know people from all over the world and it helps him practice languages.

At James' request, though, they are only speaking Spanish on this occasion:

JAMES: Hello, Damián, it is a pleasure to meet you – Hola, Damián, es un placer conocerte

*DAMIÁN: The pleasure is mine, James. Do you only have one bag? – El placer es mío, James. ¿Solo tienes **una** maleta?*

*JAMES: Yes, I am traveling light. I only have one bag but I have two… bottles of wine! – Sí, estoy viajando ligero. Solo tengo **una** maleta, pero tengo **dos**… ¡botellas de vino!*

DAMIÁN: Oh! That is great! Wait, I will show you the house first – ¡Oh! ¡Eso es genial! Espera, te mostraré la casa antes

JAMES: Sure, show me around – Claro, muéstrame

*DAMIÁN: This is the kitchen, that is the living room, and over there is the toilet. Upstairs there are four bedrooms – Esta es la cocina, esa es la sala, y aquel es el baño. Arriba hay **cuatro** habitaciones*

JAMES: Great, should we open the wine? – Genial, ¿abrimos el vino?

*DAMIÁN: Yes, but we need three glasses… because we are waiting for a guest – Sí, pero necesitamos **tres** copas… porque estamos esperando a una invitada*

Lesson 17

Right on Time!: Telling the Time and Date

Numbers are fundamental to talk about time, not only to read your watch in Spanish—if someone asks the time on the street—but also to say the day of the month, the year, to talk about your age, to say how long ago something happened... and so on.

You are going to see some examples, but first, here are the Spanish numbers up to 50:

11 – once

12 – doce

13 – trece

14 – catorce

15 – quince

16 – dieciséis

17 – diecisiete

18 – dieciocho

19 – diecinueve

20 – veinte

21 – veintiuno

22 – veintidós

23 – veintitrés

24 – veinticuatro

25 – veinticinco

26 – veintiséis

27 – veintisiete

28 – veintiocho

29 – veintinueve

30 – treinta

After 30, you write numbers with more than one word. The word *y* means *and*:

31 – treinta y uno (literally *thirty and one*)

32 – treinta y dos

33 – treinta y tres

34 – treinta y cuatro

35 – treinta y cinco

36 – treinta y seis

37 – treinta y siete

38 – treinta y ocho

39 – treinta y nueve

40 – cuarenta

41 – cuarenta y uno

42 – cuarenta y dos

43 – cuarenta y tres

44 – cuarenta y cuatro

45 – cuarenta y cinco

46 – cuarenta y seis

47 – cuarenta y siete

48 – cuarenta y ocho

49 – cuarenta y nueve

50 – cincuenta

These are some really common sentences that you will probably need to use while traveling to a Spanish-speaking country or while talking to Spanish-speaking people:

*I have been living in Spain for two years – Estoy en España hace **dos** años*

*I have been traveling for three weeks – Estoy viajando hace **tres** semanas*

*I am 28 years old – Tengo **veintiocho** años*

*I am 33 years old – Tengo **treinta y tres** años*

*I am 40 years old – Tengo **cuarenta** años*

*I was born on the 3rd of May – Nací el **tres** de mayo*

*I saw Damián five minutes ago – Vi a Damián hace **cinco** minutos*

*We are going out in **ten** minutes – Vamos a salir en **diez** minutos*

To talk about the time, first of all, you only need numbers up to 12! Even though in writing Spanish uses a 24-hour clock, when Spanish people speak, they always use the 12-hour clock. However, just like in English, they add *in the morning (de la mañana), in the afternoon (de la tarde)* and *in the evening (de la noche)* to be more precise.

When talking about some time in the morning (from 1 a.m. to 11 a.m.), Spanish people say *de la mañana*:

1 a.m. – la una de la mañana

2 a.m. – las dos de la mañana

3 a.m. – las tres de la mañana

4 a.m. – las cuatro de la mañana

5 a.m. – las cinco de la mañana

6 a.m. – las seis de la mañana

7 a.m. – las siete de la mañana

8 a.m. – las ocho de la mañana

9 a.m. – las nueve de la mañana

10 a.m. – las diez de la mañana

11 a.m. – las once de la mañana

For noon, they use *del mediodía:*

12 p.m. – las doce del mediodía

For the afternoon, they use *de la tarde*:

1 p.m. – la una de la tarde

2 p.m. – las dos de la tarde

3 p.m. – las tres de la tarde

4 p.m. – las cuatro de la tarde

5 p.m. – las cinco de la tarde

6 p.m. – las seis de la tarde

7 p.m. – las siete de la tarde (can also be considered evening)

For the evening, they say *de la noche*:

7 p.m. – las siete de la noche (can also be considered afternoon)

8 p.m. – las ocho de la noche

9 p.m. – las nueve de la noche

10 p.m. – las diez de la noche

11 p.m. – las once de la noche

For midnight, they say *medianoche*:

12 a.m. – las doce / la medianoche

In Spanish, there are not two different words for *evening* and *night*:

It's nine in the evening – Son las nueve de la noche

Tonight we are going to a restaurant – Esta noche vamos a un restaurante

I can't sleep at night – No puedo dormir por la noche

To ask for the time, ask what "hour" it is:

What time is it? – ¿Qué hora es?

To answer that question, use the verb *ser* (*to be*), always in plural, except for when it is 1 a.m. or 1 p.m., when Spanish uses the singular conjugation:

*It's three in the afternoon – **Son** las tres de la tarde*

*It's eight o'clock – **Son** las ocho en punto*

*It's one in the morning – **Es** la una de la mañana*

When it is 2:45 or 7:15, just like in English, you can say the full number or sometimes you can take some 'shortcuts':

quarter to – menos cuarto

ten to – menos diez

five to – menos cinco

o'clock – en punto

five past – y cinco

ten past – y diez

quarter past – y cuarto

half past – y media

As you can see, it is very similar to English:

2:45 – las tres menos cuarto

1:30 – la una y media

8:15 – las ocho y cuarto

5:55 – las seis menos cinco

9:50 – las diez menos diez

James is at Damián's house. They have poured the wine into three glasses, and Damián is constantly looking at the clock. James does not know what is going on:

JAMES: What time is it? – ¿Qué hora es?

DAMIÁN: It is five to four, why? – Son las cuatro menos cinco, ¿por qué?

JAMES: I do not know; what is there so interesting about the clock? - No lo sé; ¿qué es tan interesante sobre el reloj?

DAMIÁN: Oh, haha. I am waiting for someone. She is arriving at four – Oh, jaja. Estoy esperando a alguien. Ella llega a las cuatro

JAMES: Is she a friend of yours? – ¿Es una amiga tuya?

DAMIÁN: No. Well, not yet. It is a surprise – No. Bueno, no todavía. Es una sorpresa

JAMES: Are we just going to wait in silence for the next five minutes? – ¿Y solo vamos a esperar en silencio por los próximos cinco minutos?

DAMIÁN: It is not going to be necessary; here she is, right on time... – No será necesario; aquí está, justo a tiempo...

And last, but not least, to talk about time and dates you will definitely need to know the days of the week and the names of the months:

Monday – lunes

Tuesday – martes

Wednesday – miércoles

Thursday – jueves

Friday – viernes

Saturday – sábado

Sunday – domingo

January – enero

February – febrero

March – marzo

April – abril

May – mayo

June – junio

July – julio

August – agosto

September – septiembre

October – octubre

November – noviembre

December – diciembre

Lesson 18

Make History: How To Talk About Years

If you want to say the year you were born, or if you want to mention a year in which something happened, you are going to need to know how to say complex numbers like *1986* or *2001*.

It is not as hard as it seems. First, here are the thousands:

1.000 – mil

2.000 – dos mil

3.000 – tres mil

5.000 – cinco mil

15.000 – quince mil

And the hundreds:

100 – cien

200 – doscientos

300 – trescientos

400 – cuatrocientos

500 – quinientos

600 – seiscientos

700 – setecientos

800 – ochocientos

900 – novecientos

And decades:

10 – diez

20 – veinte

30 – treinta

40 – cuarenta

50 – cincuenta

60 – sesenta

70 – setenta

80 – ochenta

90 – noventa

100 – cien

Now, you just have to combine them:

1967 – mil novecientos sesenta y siete

1974 – mil novecientos setenta y cuatro

1990 – mil novecientos noventa

1999 – mil novecientos noventa y nueve

2002 – dos mil dos

2010 – dos mil diez

2019 – dos mil diecinueve

You can use the plural of thousand (*miles*) when you are talking about an unspecified amount. You can do the same with *cientos* (*hundreds*) and *millones* (millions).

*I have thousands of options – Tengo **miles** de opciones*

*Thousands of students registered – Se inscribieron **miles** de alumnos*

*In the capital, they are millions; we are hundreds of thousands – En la capital, son **millones**; nosotros somos **cientos** de **miles***

It is incorrect to say *cientas*, even when talking about something feminine:

*I have hundreds of questions – Tengo **cientos** de preguntas*

*Hundreds of women participated – Participaron **cientos** de mujeres*

Note that, in Spanish, the thousands are marked with a dot (.), not with a comma as in English. Decimals, instead, are marked with a comma. Just like in English, though, Spanish does not use the dot in some numbers, such as years.

1,500 – 1.500 (mil quinientos)

200,000 – 200.000 (doscientos mil)

1.5 – 1,5 (uno coma cinco)

2.75 – 2,75 (dos coma setenta y cinco)

year 1900 – año 1900 (mil novecientos)

The word for *million* is *millón*, but do not forget you have to say it in plural when you have more than one:

1.000.000 – un millón

2.000.000 – dos millones

10.000.000 – diez millones

(Note that, while in English, a billion is a thousand million, in Spanish, it just called a thousand millions *mil millones*. A Spanish *billón* means a million million.)

Damián gets up and walks to the door. James is really curious. He stands up and walks over to see who is at the door:

JAMES: Kate? What are you doing here? – ¿Kate? ¿Qué haces aquí?

KATE: My silly big brother, I had not seen you in years! – Mi tonto hermano mayor, ¡hacía años que no te veía!

JAMES: In two years, since you moved to Spain in 2017 – Hace dos años, desde que te mudaste a España en 2017 (dos mil diecisiete)

KATE: I bet you didn't expect to see me here now – Apuesto que no esperabas verme aquí ahora

JAMES: Of course not, it is a massive surprise. How did...? – Claro que no, es una sorpresa enorme. ¿Cómo...?

KATE: Remember you texted me three months ago telling me you were in touch with an architect from Lima? – ¿Recuerdas que me escribiste hace tres meses para decirme que estabas en contacto con un arquitecto de Lima?

JAMES: Yes, so? – Sí, ¿y?

KATE: I looked him up, I wrote him a message, and we planned all this – Lo busqué, le escribí un mensaje, y planeamos todo

Here is a list of time-related vocabulary you will definitely use while traveling around Latin America and Spain:

time – tiempo

hour – hora

minute – minuto

second – segundo

morning – mañana

noon – mediodía

afternoon – tarde

evening – noche

midnight – medianoche

night – noche

sunrise – amanecer

sunset – atardecer

today – hoy

yesterday – ayer

tomorrow – mañana

the day before yesterday – antes de ayer

the day after tomorrow – pasado mañana

now – ahora

never – nunca

always – siempre

late – tarde

early – temprano

on time – a tiempo / en horario

day – día

week – semana

month – mes

year – año

And here are some sentences where you might find these words:

I don't have much time – No tengo mucho **tiempo**

He always arrives an hour late! – ¡Siempre llega una **hora** tarde!

*I want to seize every minute – Quiero aprovechar cada **minuto***

*See you at noon – Nos vemos al **mediodía***

*We came back around midnight – Volvimos cerca de la **medianoche***

*Let's see the sunrise at the beach! – ¡Veamos el **amanecer** en la playa!*

*Let's see the sunset from the lighthouse! – ¡Veamos el **atardecer** desde el faro!*

*Today I'm leaving – **Hoy** me voy*

*I met her yesterday – La conocí **ayer***

*Have we met before? – ¿Nos conocemos de **antes**?*

*See you after work – Nos vemos **después** del trabajo*

*I went to the museum the day before yesterday – Fui al museo **antes de ayer***

*I am going to Peru the day after tomorrow – Voy a ir a Perú **pasado mañana***

*I want to do something now – Quiero hacer algo **ahora***

*I never traveled on my own – **Nunca** he viajado sola*

*She is always by my side – Ella **siempre** está a mi lado*

*I am leaving early in the morning – Me voy **temprano** por la mañana*

*My plane is leaving on time – Mi avión sale **en horario***

*This is not something you see every day – Esto no es algo que ves todos los **días***

*I'm staying for another week! – ¡Me quedo una **semana** más!*

*It was the best month of my life – Fue el mejor **mes** de mi vida*

*See you next year! – ¡Nos vemos el **año** que viene!*

Here are some tricky ones! For example, *morning* and *tomorrow* are both *mañana*:

*What a beautiful morning! – ¡Qué hermosa **mañana**!*

*I think tomorrow is going to rain – Creo que **mañana** va a llover*

And *afternoon* and *late* are both *tarde*:

*I have to work a lot this afternoon – Tengo que trabajar mucho esta **tarde***

*Do not be late – No llegues **tarde***

And remember *evening* and *night* are both *noche*:

*I do not want to go out at night – No quiero salir por la **noche***

*We are going for drinks this evening – Vamos a por unos cocktails esta **noche***

Segundo, just like in English, means both *second* (time unit) and *second* (ordinal number):

*Give me one second... – Dame un **segundo**...*

*You're the second one to ask – Eres el **segundo** en preguntar*

These are the ordinal numbers in Spanish:

1° – primero / primera

2° – segundo / segunda

3° – tercero / tercera

4° – cuarto / cuarta

5° – quinto / quinta

6° – sexto / sexta

7° – séptimo / séptima

8° – octavo / octava

9° – noveno / novena

10° – décimo / décima

Masculine ordinal numbers 1 and 3 lose the *o* when they are put before the noun they are affecting:

*I did not have many boyfriends. Alex is the first one – No tuve muchos novios. Alex es el **primero***

*Alex is my first boyfriend – Alex es mi **primer** novio*

*This day is the third of my trip – Este día es el **tercero** de mi viaje*

*It's the third day of my trip – Es mi **tercer** día de viaje*

Lesson 19

Numbers For a Rainy Day: Shopping

Numbers are not only necessary for telling the date and time, but they are in everyday life in another way as well... Maybe you even have some numbers in your pockets right now... Yes, money!

Let's take a look at local currencies and their approximate equivalent to one American dollar (this might change with time in some countries with volatile currencies, of course):

Spain: *euro* (1 American dollar is equivalent to 0.89 *euros*)

Mexico: *peso* (1 American dollar is equivalent to 19 *pesos*)

Argentina: *peso* (1 American dollar is equivalent to 45 *pesos*)

Bolivia: *boliviano* (1 American dollar is equivalent to 7 *bolivianos*)

Chile: *peso* (1 American dollar is equivalent to 663 *pesos*)

Colombia: *peso* (1 American dollar is equivalent to 3,000 *pesos*)

Paraguay: *guaraní* (1 American dollar is equivalent to 6,200 *guaraníes*)

Peru: *sol* (1 American dollar is equivalent to 3.30 *soles*)

Uruguay: *peso* (1 American dollar is equivalent to 33.80 *pesos*)

Dominican Republic: *peso* (1 American dollar is equivalent to 50 *pesos*)

Panama: *balboa* (1 American dollar is equivalent to 1 *balboa*)

Costa Rica: *colón* (1 American dollar is equivalent to 600 *colones*)

El Salvador: *colón* (1 American dollar is equivalent to 8 *colones*)

Shopping vocabulary:

cash – efectivo

credit card – tarjeta de crédito

debit card – tarjeta de débito

cash machine – cajero automático

counter – caja

the bill – la cuenta

sale – rebajas

discount – descuento

price – precio

change – vuelta / cambio

note – billete

coin – moneda

Common questions while shopping:

Do you take VISA credit cards? – ¿Aceptan tarjetas de crédito VISA?

Can I pay with cash? – ¿Puedo pagar con efectivo?

How much is it? – ¿Cuánto es?

How much is this? – ¿Cuánto cuesta esto?

What is the price for that? – ¿Cuál es el precio de eso?

How much are these two magnets? – ¿Cuánto cuestan estos dos imanes?

How much is the change? – ¿Cuánto es mi vuelto?

Some very useful verbs for ordering and buying are *querer (to want)*, *necesitar (to need)*, *dar (to give)*, *costar (to cost)*, and *ser (to be)*:

*I want three mangos and two pears – **Quiero** tres mangos y dos peras*

*I need two kilos of strawberries – **Necesito** dos kilos de fresas*

*Could I have a kilo of flour, please? – ¿Podría **darme** un kilo de harina, por favor?*

*Give me five! – ¡**Deme** cinco!*

*That costs two eighty – Eso **cuesta** dos con ochenta*

*The price is two hundred soles – El precio **es** de doscientos soles*

There is a verb you might need a lot while shopping: *pagar (to pay)*. Let's see its conjugation and some practical sentences:

Pagar (to pay)

I pay – yo pago

You pay – tú pagas / usted paga / vos pagás

He pays – él paga

She pays – ella paga

We pay – nosotros pagamos / nosotras pagamos

You pay – vosotros pagáis / vosotras pagáis / ustedes pagan

They pay – ellos pagan / ellas pagan

*I pay with cash, is it possible? – **Pago** con efectivo, ¿es posible?*

*Do we pay now? – ¿**Pagamos** ahora?*

*You pay for dinner, right? – Vosotras **pagáis** la cena, ¿verdad?*

*You pay for the coffee, I will pay por the movie tickets – Tú **pagas** el café, yo **pago** las entradas del cine*

This is basic vocabulary related to numbers:

to add – sumar

to subtract – restar

to multiply – multiplicar

to divide – dividir

the sum – la suma

the difference – la diferencia

to count – contar

The verb *contar* has two meanings! There is *contar* as in *to count*: *uno, dos, tres, cuatro*, and *contar* as in *to tell*. Let's see the conjugation and some examples:

I tell – yo cuento

You tell – tú cuentas / usted cuenta / vos contás

He tells – él cuenta

She tells – ella cuenta

We tell – nosotros contamos / nosotras contamos

You tell – vosotros contáis / vosotras contáis / ustedes cuentan

They tell – ellos cuentan / ellas cuentan

Here are some examples:

*Kate counts how many beers we have left – Kate **cuenta** cuántas cervezas tenemos*

*Sara tells me about her life – Sara me **cuenta** sobre su vida*

*Santiago tells me a secret – Santiago me **cuenta** un secreto*

*Should I tell you about my work? – ¿Te **cuento** sobre mi trabajo?*

Kate and James are very happy to see each other after so long. After having a few wines with Damián, they go to the market to buy something so they can prepare dinner:

KATE: First, how many soles do you have? – Primero, ¿cuántos soles traes?

JAMES: I have… around fifty – Tengo… unos cincuenta

KATE: Great, that'll be enough – Genial, con eso será suficiente

JAMES: Should we buy some fresh tomatoes and garlic and make pasta? – ¿Llevamos tomates frescos y ajo para hacer pasta?

KATE: Sounds perfect; how many tomatoes do we take? – Suena perfecto, ¿cuántos tomates llevamos?

JAMES: Let's take four. How much are they? – Podemos llevar cuatro. ¿Cuánto cuestan?

KATE: They are 1.20 soles per kilo. Four tomatoes are… a kilo and a half – Están a un sol con veinte cada kilo. Cuatro tomates son… ¡un kilo y medio!

JAMES: Excellent! – ¡Excelente!

Did you ever use *kilos* as a measurement unit? In Spanish-speaking countries, you will definitely use the metric system (kilograms, liters, meters, and Celsius degrees) instead of the imperial system (pounds, gallons, yards, and Fahrenheit degrees).

Let's quickly see some equivalencies:

1 kilo – 2.20 pounds

100 grams – 3.5 ounces

1 liter – 2.11 pints

4 liters – 1.05 gallons

1 meter – 3.28 feet

1 meter – 1.09 yards

1 centimeter – 0.39 inches

5 centimeters – 1.96 inches

When talking about temperature: 0 to 10 Celsius degrees is cold; 10 to 15 is chilly; 15 to 25 is warm; 25 to 30 is hot; and >30 is really hot.

0 Celsius degrees – 32 Fahrenheit degrees

15 Celsius degrees – 59 Fahrenheit degrees

30 Celsius degrees – 86 Fahrenheit degrees

What about fractions? You might need to buy half a kilo of something, or a quarter of a kilo of another thing. When you have half of something, you say "medio" or "media" depending on whether the object is masculine or feminine:

½ – *medio/media*

⅓ – *un tercio*

¼ – *un cuarto*

⅛ – *un octavo*

*Half a kilo of potatoes, please! – **Medio** kilo de patatas, ¡por favor!*

*I need half a loaf of bread – Necesito **media** hogaza de pan*

*Can I have a quarter of a kilo of strawberries, please? – ¿Podría darme **un cuarto** de kilo de fresas, por favor?*

Lesson 20

Me, Myself and I: Talking About Yourself

If you want to make friends, you have to tell your story!

In this chapter, you will read the stories of some of the characters you have met before in this book. But first, let's go over the phrases that you will need to tell your story.

Saying your name

I am James – Yo soy James

I am Damián – Soy Damián

My name is James – Me llamo James

My name is Kate – Mi nombre es Kate

My last name is Dawkins – Mi apellido es Dawkins

My full name is James Dawkins – Mi nombre completo es James Dawkins

Saying where you are from

If James and Kate want to tell other travelers or locals where they are from, these are some of the sentences they could use:

I am from England – Soy de Inglaterra

We are from Manchester, a city in England – Somos de Manchester, una ciudad de Inglaterra

We come from the United Kingdom – Venimos del Reino Unido

I am James, I am English – Soy James, soy inglés

I am Kate, I am English – Soy Kate, soy inglesa

So James and Kate are from Manchester in England! But what about other nationalities?

As you can see in the last two sentences, James says *soy inglés* and Kate says *soy inglesa*. This is because the adjective that describes your nationality may have a masculine and a feminine form; while some may just have one version (the ones ending in *e*, for example).

Also, you should not capitalize these adjectives; they should be written in the lower case.

Let's see some other examples:

I am British – Soy británico/británica

I am English – Soy inglés/inglesa

I am Scottish – Soy escocés/escocesa

I am Welsh – Soy galés/galesa

I am Australian – Soy australiano/australiana

I am Canadian – Soy canadiense (can be used for both women and men)

I am American – Soy estadounidense (can be used for both women and men)

I am Irish – Soy irlandés/irlandesa

I am French – Soy francés/francesa

I am German – Soy alemán/alemana

I am Belgian – Soy belga (can be used for both women and men)

I am Finnish – Soy finlandés/finlandesa

I am Dutch – Soy neerlandés/neerlandesa (even though this is the 'right' form, people might understand you better if you say *holandés/holandesa*)

I am Italian – Soy italiano/italiana

I am Indian – Soy indio/india

I am Japanese – Soy japonés/japonesa

I am Russian – Soy ruso/rusa

I am Swedish – Soy sueco/sueca

I am Israeli – Soy israelí (can be used for both women and men)

What about the people you meet in Latin America and Spain. What happens when they are talking about their nationalities? Here are some of the words you might hear:

I am Spanish – Soy español/española

I am Catalan – Soy catalán/catalana

I am Basque – Soy vasco/vasca

I am Argentinian – Soy argentino/argentina

I am Uruguayan – Soy uruguayo/uruguaya

I am Bolivian – Soy boliviano/boliviana

I am Brazilian – Soy brasileño/brasileña

I am Chilean – Soy chileno/chilena

I am Colombian – Soy colombiano/colombiana

I am Cuban – Soy cubano/cubana

I am Dominican – Soy dominicano/dominicana

I am Ecuadorian – Soy ecuatoriano/ecuatoriana

I am Mexican – Soy mexicano/mexicana (in this case, the *x* is pronounced as a *j*)

I am Peruvian – Soy peruano/peruana

I am Venezuelan – Soy venezolano/venezolana

You can also just say *I am from...* or *I come from...* In those cases, you will need the verb *ser*, which you have studied before, and *venir*, which means *to come*. Let's see the present tense conjugation for *venir* and some examples:

I come – yo vengo

You come – tú vienes / usted viene / vos venís

He comes – él viene

She comes – ella viene

We come – nosotros venimos / nosotras venimos

You come – vosotros venís / vosotras venís / ustedes vienen

They come – ellos vienen / ellas vienen

This is how you can use *ser* and *venir* to talk about your nationality:

*We are from the US – **Somos** de los Estados Unidos*

*We come from California, in the US – **Venimos** de California, en los Estados Unidos*

*We both come from Europe: she is from the Netherlands, I am from Belgium – Las dos **venimos** de Europa: ella **es** de los Países Bajos, yo **soy** de Bélgica*

But wait, life is more complex than this! People travel, they move, they gain new nationalities, they have kids with people from other countries, they move again.

In the current globalized world, just learning how to say *I am French* is of no use. Let's see some of the sentences you might need to say, or you might hear while traveling:

I'm half French, half American. My mother is French; my father is from New York – Soy mitad francés, mitad estadounidense. Mi madre es francesa; mi padre es de Nueva York

I am Japanese, but I come from the UK – Soy japonesa, pero vengo del Reino Unido

My parents are from India, but I identify as English – Mis padres son de la India, pero yo me identifico como inglés

I am from the US, but I've been living in Spain for two years now – Soy de los Estados Unidos, pero llevo viviendo dos años en España

I am originally from a small town near Toronto, but now I live in Montreal – Soy originalmente de un pequeño pueblo cerca de Toronto, pero ahora vivo en Montreal

My father is Venezuelan, and my mother is English, I was born and raised in Canada, but now I live in New York! – Mi padre es venezolano, y mi mamá es inglesa, nací y crecí en Canadá, ¡pero ahora vivo en Nueva York!

Sounds more like real life, right? In the next lesson, you will learn some more vocabulary to talk about families.

Lesson 21

It's All Relative: Talk About Your Family

When you travel, it is normal for people to ask about your family. Do you have brothers or sisters? Where do your parents live? Are you married?

First of all, let's start with the basic relative-related vocabulary:

mother – madre

mom – mamá

father – padre

dad – papá

brother – hermano

sister – hermana

grandmother – abuela

grandfather – abuelo

cousin – primo/prima

uncle – tío

aunt – tía

To make the plural out of any of these words, you just have to add an *s* at the end.

Let's see some examples:

My parents call me everyday – Mis padres me llaman todos los días

We are cousins; our moms are sisters – Somos primos; nuestras mamás son hermanas

My brothers are traveling with me – Mis hermanos están viajando conmigo

My uncle and aunt will come visit soon – Mis tíos vendrán de visita pronto

Families can be much bigger than this though! Let's see some of the family members that are not necessarily blood-related:

girlfriend – novia

boyfriend – novio

partner – pareja

husband – esposo

wife – esposa

stepmom – madrastra

stepdad – padrastro

stepbrother – hermanastro

stepsister – hermanastra

half-brother – medio hermano

half-sister – medio hermana

stepson – hijastro

stepdaughter – hijastra

brother-in-law – cuñado

sister-in-law – cuñada

mother-in-law – suegra

father-in-law – suegro

son-in-law – yerno

daughter-in-law – nuera

Let's see some examples of useful sentences to talk about your family:

I have my mom, my dad, two brothers and two sisters – Tengo a mi mamá, mi papá, dos hermanos y dos hermanas

I am the youngest – Soy el más joven

I am the oldest – Soy el mayor

I am the middle child – Soy el del medio

I live with my parents – Vivo con mis padres

I live with my brother – Vivo con mi hermano

My parents are divorced – Mis padres están divorciados

My parents are not together – Mis padres no están juntos

I am married – Estoy casado / casada

I have a boyfriend – Tengo novio

I have a girlfriend – Tengo novia

Wow! That's a big family. However, there is still some missing… Pets! Here are some animal names:

dog – perro

cat – gato

fish – pez

turtle – tortuga

bird – pájaro

James and Kate go back to Damián's house where they cook some pasta for the three of them. At dinner, they tell Damián about their family:

KATE: Our dad is half Irish, but he grew up in Liverpool – <u>Nuestro</u> padre es medio irlandés, pero creció en Liverpool

JAMES: Our mom is Welsh, but she moved to Manchester when she was a kid – <u>Nuestra</u> madre es galesa, pero se mudó a Manchester cuando era una niña

DAMIÁN: Were you both born in Manchester? – ¿Nacisteis ambos en Manchester?

KATE: Yes. I moved to London to study when I was 17, and now I've been living in Palma for two years – Sí. Me mudé a Londres para estudiar a los 17 años, y ahora estoy viviendo en Palma hace dos años

JAMES: What is your story, Damián? – ¿Cuál es <u>tu</u> historia, Damián?

DAMIÁN: My mother is Bolivian; my father is Peruvian - <u>Mi</u> madre es boliviana; <u>mi</u> padre es peruano

JAMES: Did your parents meet here? – ¿<u>Tus</u> padres se conocieron aquí?

DAMIÁN: No, they met in Argentina. I grew up there, but my heart is here – No, se conocieron en Argentina. Yo crecí allí, pero <u>mi</u> corazón está aquí

There are some words in the last conversation to notice: *mi, tu, nuestro, nuestra, tus*. These are all possessive pronouns.

Just like in English, in Spanish, there are two kinds of possessive pronouns:

*My book – **Mi** libro*

*The book is mine – El libro es **mío***

The only big difference is that Spanish has plural possessive pronouns for when you are talking about more than one possession:

*My books – **Mis** libros*

*The books are mine – Los libros son **míos***

The first kind of possessives are the ones you always have to put *before* the object:

my – mi

your – tu (for *tú* and *vos*) / *su* (for *usted*)

his/her – su

our – nuestro / nuestra

your – vuestro / vuestra (for *vosotros* and *vosotras*) / *su* (for *ustedes*)

their – su

In the cases of *nuestro, nuestra, vuestro,* and *vuestra,* the 'gender' changes according to the object, not the owners:

*That is our house – Esa es **nuestra** casa*

*Our car is red – **Nuestro** auto es rojo*

*Your daughters are very tall – **Vuestras** hijas son muy altas*

These are the plurals for these possessive pronouns:

my – mis

your – tus / sus

his/her – sus

our – nuestros / nuestras

your – vuestros / vuestras / sus

their – sus

Here are some sentences where you might find these pronouns:

*My house is around the corner – **Mi** casa está a la vuelta de la esquina*

*My friends are always there for me – **Mis** amigos están siempre para mí*

*May I borrow your notebook? – ¿Me prestas **tu** cuaderno?*

*May I borrow your notes? – ¿Me prestas **tus** apuntes?*

*I love her hair – Amo **su** cabello*

*I don't care about her problems – No me interesan **sus** problemas*

*You are always welcome in our home – Siempre serás bienvenido en **nuestro** hogar*

*You'll always be in our thoughts – Siempre estarás en **nuestros** pensamientos*

*Your service improves every day – **Vuestro** servicio mejora todos los días*

*Your clients never complain – **Vuestros** clientes jamás se quejan*

*Their problem is their lack of training – **Su** problema es la falta de entrenamiento*

*I love their uniforms! – ¡Amo **sus** uniformes!*

These are the possessive pronouns of the second kind, which you normally put *after* the object and the verb:

mine – mío / mía

yours – tuyo / tuya /suyo / suya

his/hers – suyo / suya

ours – nuestro / nuestra

yours – vuestro / vuestra / suyo / suya

theirs – suyo / suya

And these are their plurals:

mine – míos / mías

yours – tuyos / tuyas

his/hers – suyos / suyas

ours – nuestros / nuestras

yours – vuestros / vuestras / suyos / suyas

theirs – suyos / suyas

Here are some sentences where you might find these pronouns:

*The car is mine – El auto es **mío***

*The ideas are mine – Las ideas son **mías***

*The world is yours – El mundo es **tuyo***

*Are these trousers yours? – ¿Estos pantalones son **tuyos**?*

*The song wasn't hers – La canción no era **suya***

*The benefits are his – Los beneficios son **suyos***

*The fault is ours – La culpa es **nuestra***

*The responsibilities are ours – Las responsabilidades son **nuestras***

*The result is yours – El resultado es **vuestro***

*The leftovers are yours – Las sobras son **vuestras***

*Their love is only theirs – Su amor es **suyo***

*The children are theirs – Los hijos son **suyos***

Lesson 22

Study and work

Now, you will look at some subjects that might be useful regarding discussing your academic and professional life, getting to know others, and building professional links.

First of all, let's start with some very important verbs when it comes to academic life: *estudiar (to study), enseñar (to teach), escribir (to write),* and *trabajar (to work).*

Estudiar (to study)

I study – yo estudio

You study – tú estudias / usted estudia / vos estudiás

He studies – él estudia

She studies – ella estudia

We study – nosotros estudiamos / nosotras estudiamos

You study – vosotros estudiáis / vosotras estudiáis / ustedes estudian

They study – ellos estudian / ellas estudian

Enseñar (to teach)

I teach – yo enseño

You teach – tú enseñas / usted enseña / vos enseñás

He teaches – él enseña

She teaches – ella enseña

We teach – nosotros enseñamos / nosotras enseñamos

You teach – vosotros enseñáis / vosotras enseñáis / ustedes enseñan

They teach – ellos enseñan / ellas enseñan

Escribir (to write)

I write – yo escribo

You write – tú escribes / usted escribe / vos escribís

He writes – él escribe

She writes – ella escribe

We write – nosotros escribimos / nosotras escribimos

You write – vosotros escribís / vosotras escribís / ustedes escriben

They write – ellos escriben / ellas escriben

Trabajar (to work)

I work – yo trabajo

You work – tú trabajas / usted trabaja / vos trabajás

He works – él trabaja

She works – ella trabaja

We work – nosotros trabajamos / nosotras trabajamos

You work – vosotros trabajáis / vosotras trabajáis / ustedes trabajan

They work – ellos trabajan / ellas trabajan

Here are some sentences where you can use these verbs when getting to know people:

*I work in a bank – Yo **trabajo** en un banco*

My brother and I work at my mother's restaurant – *Mi hermano y yo* **trabajamos** *en el restaurante de nuestra madre*

I do not work; I only study – *No* **trabajo**; *solo* **estudio**

I study at Dortmund's University – **Estudio** *en la universidad de Dortmund*

I am studying Medicine – **Estoy estudiando** *Medicina*

I am studying to be a chef – **Estoy estudiando** *para ser cocinera*

I study and work at the same time – **Estudio** *y* **trabajo** *al mismo tiempo*

My sister studies law – *Mi hermana* **estudia** *Derecho*

Those guys work at a nearby coffee shop – *Esos muchachos* **trabajan** *en un café cerca de aquí*

We are working on a new project – **Estamos trabajando** *en un nuevo proyecto*

Tomorrow I'm working the whole day – *Mañana* **trabajo** *todo el día*

Where do you work? – *¿En dónde* **trabajas***?*

What do you do for work? – *¿De qué* **trabajas***?*

María, from the hostel in Cartagena, has quite an interesting academic and professional story.

María's story:

Soy María Castro. Tengo 22 años. Estoy estudiando hotelería y turismo—por eso viajo mucho.

I am María Castro. I am 22 years old. I am studying hospitality and tourism—that's why I travel a lot.

Soy de Bogotá, pero ahora estoy viajando por toda Colombia. Debo conocer bien mi país si quiero trabajar en turismo.

I am from Bogotá, but now I'm traveling all around Colombia. I have to know my country well if I want to work in tourism.

También conozco otros países de Latinoamérica: Brasil, Ecuador, República Dominicana, Panamá, Uruguay, Surinam, Venezuela. Y conozco Estados Unidos y Europa.

I also know other countries in Latin America: Brasil, Ecuador, Dominican Republic, Panama, Uruguay, Surinam, Venezuela. And I know the United States and Europe.

En mi último viaje a Europa conocí a Alex. Nos enamoramos desde el primer día que nos conocimos, y desde ese momento me sigue para todos lados. Él es diseñador gráfico freelance, así que puede trabajar en cualquier sitio.

On my last trip to Europe I met Alex. We fell in love since the first day we met, and from that moment on he's been following me around everywhere I go. He's a freelance graphic designer, so he can travel anywhere.

Me parece genial tener una pareja que pueda viajar conmigo. Mi último novio era contador, y siempre que yo quería viajar era un problema porque él solo tenía dos semanas de vacaciones al año.

I think it's cool to have a partner that can travel with me. My last boyfriend was an accountant, and every time I wanted to travel, it was a problem because he only had two weeks of holiday every year.

But what about the past? What if you have finished with your studies or you changed jobs. The goal is not to overwhelm you with complicated past tense conjugations, but here are some examples of sentences you might need to express what was and no longer is:

I studied many things in University – **Estudié** *muchas cosas en la universidad*

I used to work too much; now I work less – Antes **trabajaba** *demasiado; ahora* **trabajo** *menos*

I used to study Literature, but now I study Marketing – **Estudiaba** *Literatura, pero ahora* **estudio** *Marketing*

I worked for three years in a big company – **Trabajé** *durante 3 años en una gran empresa*

I used to work at my town's McDonald's, and now I own my own company – *Antes* **trabajaba** *en el McDonald's de mi pueblo, y ahora tengo mi propia empresa*

Lesson 23

The Past: Guess What Happened?

In the last lesson, you saw some examples of the past tenses. Now, they are going to be detailed further. To learn the different past tenses, you are going to use the *-ar, -er, -ir* model verbs in Spanish, which are *amar (to love), temer (to fear),* and *vivir (to live).*

Pretérito perfecto simple

This verbal tense is a past tense equivalent to the English simple past: *I loved, I feared, I lived.*

To love (*amar*)

*I loved – yo am**é***

*You loved – tú am**aste** / vos am**aste** / usted am**ó***

*He loved – él am**ó***

*She loved – ella am**ó***

*We loved – nosotros am**amos** / nosotras am**amos***

*You loved – vosotros am**asteis** / vosotras am**asteis** / ustedes am**aron***

*They loved – ellos ama**ron** / ellas ama**ron***

To fear (temer)

*I feared – yo tem**í***

*You feared – tú tem**iste** / vos tem**iste** / usted tem**ió***

*He feared – él tem**ió***

*She feared – ella tem**ió***

*We feared – nosotros tem**imos** / nosotras tem**imos***

*You feared – vosotros tem**isteis** / vosotras tem**isteis** / ustedes tem**ieron***

*They feared – ellos tem**ieron** / ellas tem**ieron***

To live (vivir)

*I lived – yo viv**í***

*You lived – tú viv**iste** / vos viv**iste** / usted viv**ió***

*He lived – él viv**ió***

*She lived – ella viv**ió***

*We lived – nosotros viv**imos** / nosotras viv**imos***

*You lived – vosotros viv**isteis** / vosotras viv**isteis** / ustedes vivieron*

*They lived – ellos viv**ieron** / ellas viv**ieron***

Let's see some sentences where you could use some regular verbs conjugated in this tense:

*I bought a car – Yo **compré** un auto*

*Martina and Juana ate a whole pizza – Martina y Juana **comieron** toda la pizza*

*We wrote a book – Nosotros **escribimos** un libro*

Pretérito perfecto compuesto

This past tense is widely used and is equivalent to the English present perfect: *I have loved, I have feared, I have lived*. Instead of using the verb *to have*, Spanish uses a special verb that is only used in this occasion: *haber*. While *haber* is conjugated, the verb remains the same:

To love (amar)

yo **he** am**ado**

tú **has** am**ado** / vos **has** am**ado** / usted **ha** am**ado**

él/ella **ha** am**ado**

nosotros/as **hemos** am**ado**

ustedes han am**ado** / vosotros/as **habéis** am**ado**

ellos/ellas **han** am**ado**

To fear (temer)

yo **he** tem**ido**

tú **has** tem**ido** / vos **has** tem**ido** / usted **ha** tem**ido**

él/ella **ha** tem**ido**

nosotros/as **hemos** tem**ido**

ustedes **han** tem**ido** / vosotros/as **habéis** tem**ido**

ellos/ellas **han** tem**ido**

To live (vivir)

yo **he** viv**ido**

tú **has** viv**ido** / vos **has** viv**ido** / usted **ha** viv**ido**

él/ella **ha** viv**ido**

nosotros/as **hemos** viv**ido**

ustedes **han** viv**ido** / vosotros/as **habéis** viv**ido**

ellos/ellas **han** viv**ido**

Let's see some sentences where you could use some regular verbs conjugated in this tense:

*Who has taken my things? – ¿Quién **ha tomado** mis cosas?*

We have drunk the whole bottle – **Hemos bebido** *toda la botella*

My parents have forbidden us to go out – *Mis padres nos* **han prohibido** *salir*

Pretérito imperfecto

This verbal tense is sometimes confusing to English-speaking people because it is also equivalent to the English simple past, but it also works as the past continuous: *I was loving, I was fearing, I was living*. It is a bit of both since it expresses a continuity in a past action:

To love (amar)

yo am**aba**

tú am**abas** / vos am**abas** / usted am**aba**

él/ella am**aba**

nosotros/as am**ábamos**

ustedes am**aban** / vosotros/as am**abais**

ellos/ellas am**aban**

To fear (temer)

yo tem**ía**

tú tem**ías** / vos tem**ías** / usted tem**ía**

él/ella tem**ía**

nosotros/as tem**íamos**

ustedes tem**ían** / vosotros/as tem**íais**

ellos/ellas tem**ían**

To live (vivir)

yo viv**ía**

tú viv**ías** / vos viv**ías** / usted viv**ía**

él/ella viv**ía**

nosotros/as viv**íamos**

ustedes viv**ía** / vosotros/as viv**íais**

ellos/ellas viv**ían**

Let's see some sentences where you could use some regular verbs conjugated in this tense:

*When I was a kid, I loved cartoons – De niña, **amaba** los dibujos animados*

*My grandparents always walked around the park holding hands – Mis abuelos siempre **recorrían** el parque de la mano*

*I always used to receive the same Christmas gift: socks! – Siempre **recibía** el mismo regalo en Navidad: ¡calcetines!*

Do you remember Alex, María's boyfriend? He has practiced a lot of Spanish, and his past tenses are in quite good shape. Here is his story:

Soy Alex. Soy australiano, de Perth. Nací en Sydney, en realidad, pero mi papá era minero, así que nos mudamos todos a Perth cuando yo era un niño.

I'm Alex. I'm Australian, from Perth. I was born in Sydney, actually, but my dad was a miner, so we all moved to Perth when I was a kid.

No planeaba vivir aquí en Sudamérica. Ni siquiera planeaba viajar aquí en un inicio. Pero me enamoré…

I didn't plan on living here in South America. I didn't even plan to travel here in the first place. But I fell in love…

Conocí a María en España. Había tomado algunas clases de español en Australia, y decidí viajar a España para practicar y conocer la cultura española.

I met María in Spain. I had taken some Spanish lessons back in Australia, and I decided to travel to Spain so I could practice and get to know the Spanish culture.

En mi primer día en Europa, cuando hice el check-in en el hostal en Madrid, ahí estaba ella. Era muy temprano por la mañana, cerca de las cinco. Ella estaba tomando un café y leyendo un libro en la sala. "No puedo dormer," dijo.

On my first day in Europe, when I checked in at the hostel in Madrid, there she was. It was really early in the morning, around five. She was having a coffee and reading a book in the common room. "I can't sleep," she said.

Aunque yo estaba muy cansado después de volar por más de 20 horas, me quedé allí con ella. Hablamos por horas. Luego de tomar una ducha, salimos a caminar, y ella me mostró la ciudad.

Even though I was really tired after flying for more than twenty hours, I stayed there with her. We talked for hours. After taking a shower, we went out for a walk, and she showed me the city.

Y eso fue todo. Pasamos todo un mes en España juntos. Luego, ella debía regresar a Colombia, así que yo dije "¿Puedo ir contigo?". Ella dijo "¡No creo que a mi esposo le guste eso!". Estaba bromeando, por supuesto. Así que ahora estamos aquí.

And that was it. We spent a whole month in Spain together. Then, she had to come back to Colombia, so I said, "Can I come with you?" She said, "I don't think my husband will like that!" She was joking, of course. So now we're here.

Lesson 24

Nomad Talk: All About Traveling

Kate and James love Lima. They are staying there, at Damián's house, for a week. They talk to a lot of backpackers and local people. Every time they meet someone, they find themselves asking and answering the same things over and over again.

These are some of the questions they hear all the time and their answers:

Where are you two from? – ¿De dónde son?

KATE: We are from England – Somos de Inglaterra

Are you traveling together? – ¿Están <u>viajando</u> juntos?

JAMES: Yes, we are traveling together; we are brother and sister – Sí, estamos viajando juntos; somos hermanos

Who is older? – ¿Quién es el mayor?

JAMES: I am; she is two years younger – Yo; Ella es dos años menor

For how long? – ¿Durante cuánto tiempo?

JAMES: My sister is traveling just for a few weeks – *Mi hermana solo está viajando por un par de semanas*

And you? – *¿Y tú?*

JAMES: I don't know – *Yo no lo sé*

What do you do? – *¿A qué te dedicas?*

KATE: I am a chef – *Soy chef*

Do you work in a restaurant? – *¿Trabajas en un restaurante?*

KATE: No, I work on yachts and cruises – *No, trabajo en yates y cruceros*

What do you do, James? – *¿Tú qué haces, James?*

JAMES: I want to be a travel journalist, but first I want to learn Spanish – *Quiero ser un periodista de viajes, pero antes debo aprender español*

Your Spanish is very good – *Tu español es muy bueno*

JAMES: Thanks a lot! That is a lie, but thank you – *Muchas gracias. Es mentira, pero gracias*

For how long have you been traveling? – *¿Cuánto tiempo llevas viajando?*

JAMES: I've been traveling for a month – *Estoy viajando hace un mes*

Which countries are you visiting? – *¿Qué países <u>visitarás</u>?*

JAMES: I have been to Colombia, and now Peru. Afterward, we are going to Chile. Then, I am going to Argentina on my own, and then I do not know – *He estado en Colombia y, ahora, en Perú. Después vamos a Chile. Más adelante, voy a Argentina solo y luego no lo sé*

Are you going back to England? – *¿Tú vuelves a Inglaterra?*

KATE: No, I live in Spain, in Palma – *No, vivo en España, en Palma*

Do you like Spain? - *¿Te gusta España?*

KATE: I love Spain. It is a beautiful country, and people are great –
Amo España. Es un país hermoso, y la gente es genial

What would you like to see in Chile? – ¿Qué les gustaría ver en Chile?

KATE AND JAMES: Everything! – ¡Todo!

When you are traveling, you move a lot, right? Let's see some vocabulary and sentences related to transportation that you might need for your trip:

Public transport

You will probably use public transport to move around, or you may go for a walk and need help reaching your destination. Either way, you should remember a few simple questions to ask for directions, buy tickets, or find your way around. If you can tell people where you want to go, you should find your way with a little luck. Even if you do not understand, these phrases will help you direct your taxi drivers and get rudimentary advice from people on the street:

bus – bus

train – tren

bicycle – bicicleta

taxi – taxi

ticket – boleto / billete / pasaje

single ticket – boleto de ida

return ticket – boleto ida y vuelta

luggage – equipaje

bag – maleta

backpack – mochila

train station – estación de trenes

bus station – estación de buses

Here are some sentences that will help you get to your destination as soon as possible:

When is the next train to the main station? – ¿Cuándo viene el próximo tren hacia la estación central?

From which track is this train departing? – ¿Desde qué andén parte este tren?

Which ticket/price level do I need to go to this stop? – ¿Qué pasaje necesito para ir hasta esta parada?

The train is 10 minutes late – El tren tiene un retraso de 10 minutos

Is this seat free? – ¿Este asiento está libre?

How much is a ticket to Rivadavia Street? – ¿Cuánto cuesta un pasaje/boleto/billete a la calle Rivadavia?

Can I pay on the bus? – ¿Puedo pagar en el bus?

One ticket to Bicentenario park, please – Un pasaje al parque Bicentenario, por favor

Where does this train/bus go? – ¿A dónde va este tren/bus?

Where does the bus to Miraflores stop? – ¿Dónde para el bus a Miraflores?

When is the bus to Miraflores leaving? – ¿Cuándo parte el bus a Miraflores?

Does this bus stop at Miraflores? – ¿Se detiene este bus en Miraflores?

Where's the ticket office? – ¿Dónde está la boletería?

Where are the ticket machines? – ¿Dónde están las máquinas de boletos?

What time's the next bus to Lima? – ¿Cuándo parte el próximo bus a Lima?

How much is a ticket to Santiago? – ¿Cuánto cuesta un boleto a Santiago?

Are there buses to Santiago? – ¿Hay buses a Santiago?

The flight got canceled – El vuelo se canceló

Now let's see how to conjugate the above verbs in the present tense:

Viajar (to travel)

I travel – yo viajo

You travel – tú viajas / usted viaja / vos viajás

He travels – él viaja

She travels – ella viaja

We travel – nosotros viajamos / nosotras viajamos

You travel – vosotros viajáis / vosotras viajáis / ustedes viajan

They travel – ellos viajan / ellas viajan

Here are some practical examples with the verb *viajar*:

I save money for nine months and then I travel for three months – Ahorro dinero por nueve meses y luego viajo por tres meses

My sister is traveling around the world – Mi hermana está viajando por todo el mundo

My boyfriend and me, we travel every year to a new place – Mi novio y yo viajamos a un lugar nuevo todos los años

James travels around Latin America – James viaja por Latinoamérica

My parents never travel – Mis padres nunca viajan

Visitar (to visit)

I visit – yo visito

You visit – tú visitas / usted visita / vos visitás

He visits – él visita

She visits – ella visita

We visit – nosotros visitamos / nosotras visitamos

You visit – vosotros visitáis / vosotras visitáis / ustedes visitan

They visit – ellos visitan / ellas visitan

Here are some practical examples with the verb *visitar*:

*We visit Chile with my sister – **Visitamos** Chile con mi hermana*

*My mother visits me in Spain whenever she can – Mi madre me **visita** en España cuando puede*

*Why do you visit every museum if you do not like art? – ¿Por qué **visitas** todos los museos si no te gusta el arte?*

Venir (to come)

I come – yo vengo

You come – tú vienes / usted viene / vos venís

He comes – él viene

She comes – ella viene

We come – nosotros venimos / nosotras venimos

You come – vosotros venís / vosotras venís / ustedes vienen

They come – ellos vienen / ellas vienen

Here are some practical examples with the verb *venir*:

*I come from England – **Vengo** de Inglaterra*

*The train is coming late – El tren **viene** con retraso*

*My parents are coming to visit – Mis padres **vienen** de visita*

*We come from afar – **Venimos** de muy lejos*

*They come here every year – Ellas **vienen** aquí todos los años*

Partir (to depart)

I depart – yo parto

You depart – tú partes / usted parte / vos partís

He departs – él parte

She departs – ella parte

We depart – nosotros partimos / nosotras partimos

You depart – vosotros partís / vosotras partís / ustedes parten

They depart – ellos parten / ellas parten

Here are some practical examples with the verb *partir*:

I am sad; I depart tomorrow – Estoy triste; parto mañana

My plane is departing from Cartagena's Airport – Mi avión parte del Aeropuerto de Cartagena

The train is departing from track number three – El tren parte del tercer andén

After dinner, we depart to the station – Luego de la cena, partimos para la estación

I love this place; I do not want to depart – Amo este lugar; no quiero partir

Asking for directions

It is very probable that, eventually, if you need to get from point A to point B, you will need to ask for directions in Spanish. Here are some practical sentences you might need while lost or asking for directions:

I am lost – Estoy perdido / perdida

How do I get to the train station? – ¿Cómo llego a la estación de tren?

Do you know this hotel? – ¿Conoces este hotel?

Can you show me on the map? – ¿Me lo puede mostrar en el mapa?

These are some of the answers you might hear:

Go straight – Ve todo recto

Continue straight – Sigue todo recto

Turn right – Dobla a la derecha

Turn left – Dobla a la izquierda

Stop – Detente

Turn – Gira

Cross the street – Cruza la calle

Cross the park – Atraviesa el parque

After the bridge – Después del puente

Before the main square – Antes de la plaza principal

It is in front of the sea – Está enfrente del mar

It is in front of a big building – Está frente a un gran edificio

After two blocks, turn to the left – Después de dos calles, gira a la izquierda

Vocabulary for touristic activities

Theatre

¿Hay algo en el teatro...? – Is there anything on at the theatre...?

Esta noche – tonight

Esta semana – this week

Este mes – this month

¿Hasta cuándo está la obra? – When's the play on until?

¿Quién actúa? – Who's in it?

¿Qué tipo de producción es? – What type of production is it?

Es... – It's...

Una comedia – a comedy

Una tragedia – a tragedy

Un musical – a musical

Una ópera – an opera

Un ballet – a ballet

¿La has visto antes? – Have you seen it before?

¿A qué hora comienza el espectáculo? – What time does the performance start?

¿A qué hora termina? – What time does it finish?

¿Dónde está el guardarropa? – Where's the cloakroom?

¿Deseas un programa? – Would you like a program?

¿Puede darme un programa, por favor? – Could I have a program, please?

¿Pedimos unos tragos para el entreacto? – Shall we order some drinks for the interval?

Deberíamos volver a nuestros asientos – We'd better go back to our seats

¿Te ha gustado? – Did you enjoy it?

The club

¿Quieres ir a un club/una discoteca esta noche? – Do you want to go to a club tonight?

¿Hay alguna buena discoteca en esta zona? – Do you know any good clubs near here?

¿Hasta qué hora abre? – Until what time is it open?

¿A qué hora cierran? – What time do they close?

¿Cuánto cuesta la entrada? – How much is it to get in?

¿Hay un código de vestimenta? – Is there a dress code?

¿Qué noches abren? – What nights are you open?

¿Qué tipo de música es? – What sort of music is it?

¿Qué hay esta noche? – What's on tonight?

¿Hay música en vivo esta noche? – Is there any live music tonight?

Disculpe, no puede entrar – Sorry, you can't come in

No puede entrar con zapatillas – You can't come in with trainers on

Hay una fiesta privada esta noche – There's a private party tonight

El club está lleno – The club's full

Estoy en la lista de invitados – I'm on the guest list

Soy miembro – I'm a member

¿Dónde está el guardarropa? – Where's the cloakroom?

¿Qué piensas del DJ? – What do you think of the DJ?

¡La música es genial! – The music's great!

Está un poco vacío – It's a bit empty

¿Dónde está el bar? – Where's the bar?

Hay una larga fila en el bar – There's a long queue at the bar

Está demasiado ruidoso – It's too loud

Hace demasiado calor aquí – It's too hot in here

¿Estás listo/a para ir a casa? – Are you ready to go home?

Me voy a casa – I'm going home

Leisure and art

¿Cuánto cuesta la entrada? – How much is it to get in?

¿Hay un costo de admisión? – Is there an admission charge?

Solo para la exhibición – Only for the exhibition

¿A qué hora cierran? – What time do they close?

El museo cierra los lunes – The museum's closed on Mondays

¿Puedo tomar fotografías? – Can I take photographs?

¿Le gustaría una audioguía? – Would you like an audio-guide?

¿Hay visitas guiadas el día de hoy? – Are there any guided tours today?

¿A qué hora comienza la próxima visita guiada? – What time does the next guided tour start?

¿Dónde está el guardarropa? – Where's the cloakroom?

Tenemos que dejar nuestros bolsos en el guardarropa – We have to leave our bags in the cloakroom

¿Tiene un plano del museo? – Do you have a plan of the museum?

¿Quién pintó este cuadro? – Who's this painting by?

Este museo tiene una buena colección de… – This museum's got a very good collection of…

Pinturas al óleo – oil paintings

Acuarelas – watercolors

Retratos – portraits

Paisajes – landscapes

Esculturas – sculptures

Artefactos antiguos – ancient artifacts

Cerámica – pottery

¿Te gusta…? – Do you like…?

El arte moderno – modern art

Las pinturas clásicas – classical paintings

Las pinturas impresionistas – impressionist paintings

Plaza – square

Parque – park

Calle – street

Panadería/pastelería – bakery

Tienda de libros/librería – bookshop

Tienda de ropa – clothes shop

Floristería – florists

Tienda de regalos – gift shop

Juguetería – toy shop

Galería de arte – art gallery

Banco – bank

Bar – bar

Café – café

Catedral – cathedral

Iglesia – church

Cine – cinema

Sala de conciertos – concert hall

Gimnasio – gym

Biblioteca – library

Museo – museum

Centro de compras – shopping center

Teatro – theatre

Cementerio – cemetery

Mercado – marketplace

Estadio – stadium

Zoológico – zoo

Ruinas – ruins

Lesson 25

Using Prepositions To Tell Your Story

This book will not bore you with a long list of Spanish prepositions—most of which you might never use.

Instead, a short text written by Kate and James is provided. In this text, they explain who they are, when they were born, where they are from, where they live, and something about their family.

Afterward, the prepositions they used will be clarified so that you can learn how to use them like a local. To make it a bit more difficult, the Spanish version is first, and the English version is second.

Kate's story:

¡Hola! Me llamo Kate Dawkins; soy la hermana <u>de</u> James. Actualmente vivo <u>en</u> España, <u>por</u> lo que mi español es mucho mejor que el suyo. Jaja, solo bromeo… igual es cierto.

Hello! My name is Kate Dawkins; I'm James' sister. I currently live in Spain, and that's why my Spanish is much better than his. Haha, just joking… It's true though.

Tengo 26 años. Nací en el 1993. Soy la más joven de la familia. Tenemos otro hermano, que tiene 30, y luego está mi hermana mayor, que tiene 35.

I'm 26 years old. I was born in 1993. I'm the youngest in our family. We have another brother, who's 30, and then there's my older sister, who's 35.

Mi mamá es ingeniera. Tiene 55 años, y aún trabaja mucho. No quiere retirarse pronto. Mi padre era investigador, pero está retirado. Están divorciados, pero son buenos amigos.

My mom is an engineer. She's 55 years old, and she still works a lot. She doesn't want to retire soon. My father was a researcher, but he's retired. They are divorced, but they are good friends.

Vivo en España, en Palma de Mallorca, hace dos años... Bueno, realmente no vivo en Palma; ¡paso casi todo mi tiempo en el mar! En Inglaterra, estudié para ser chef. Actualmente trabajo en distintos barcos y cruceros.

I've lived in Spain, in Palma de Mallorca, for two years... Well, I don't really live in Palma; I spend most of my time at the sea! In England, I studied to be a chef. I currently work on different boats and cruises.

Me gusta mucho cocinar, y me gusta mucho trabajar en el mar. El único problema es que no puedo tener una mascota...

I love cooking, and I love working at sea. The only problem is that I cannot have a pet...

En un tiempo, cuando ahorre el dinero suficiente, me gustaría hacer una pasantía en un restaurante con estrellas Michelin.

In a while, when I save enough money, I'd love to do an internship at a Michelin-star restaurant.

James' story:

Hola a todos. Me llamo James. Bueno, mi nombre completo es James Dawkins. Tengo 28 años. Nací el 12 de diciembre de 1991.

Hello, everyone. My name is James. Well, my full name is James Dawkins. I am 28 years old. I was born on the 12th of December 1991.

Siempre me gustó escribir. Amo escribir. Escribo <u>sobre</u> todo lo que veo. Generalmente escribo <u>en</u> inglés, pero ahora también estoy aprendiendo <u>a</u> escribir <u>en</u> español.

I always liked writing. I love writing. I write about everything I see. I generally write in English, but now I'm also learning to write in Spanish.

Empecé <u>a</u> aprender español hace dos años. Tomé un curso <u>en</u> la universidad, mientras estudiaba periodismo. Me gustaría hacer periodismo <u>de</u> viajes... o periodismo internacional. <u>Por</u> eso, creo que es muy importante que aprenda español muy bien.

I started learning Spanish two years ago. I took a Spanish course in university, while I was studying journalism. I would like to do travel journalism... or international journalism. Because of that, I think it's very important that I learn how to speak Spanish well.

Estoy viajando <u>por</u> Sudamérica <u>desde</u> hace dos meses. El primer mes lo pasé <u>en</u> Colombia. Ahora estoy <u>en</u> Perú. Me gusta mucho el clima de Lima; es mucho mejor que el clima <u>de</u> Cartagena.

I've been traveling around South America for two months. The first month I spent it in Colombia. Now I'm in Peru. I like Lima's weather a lot; it's much better that Cartagena's weather.

El próximo país que visitaré será Chile. Luego iré <u>a</u> Argentina, Uruguay, Brasil... Estoy muy emocionado. <u>Hasta</u> ahora, todas las personas que he conocido han sido geniales conmigo. Tengo muchos amigos nuevos.

The next country I'm traveling to is going to be Chile. Afterward I'll go to Argentina, Uruguay, Brazil... I'm very excited. Until now, every person I've met has been great with me. I have many new friends.

Let's see what prepositions Kate and James used to tell their stories:

De (of, from)

De indicates possession or belonging:

*I'm James' sister – Soy la hermana **de** James*

*I'm the youngest in our family – Soy la más joven **de** la familia*

*Lima's weather is better that Cartagena's – El clima **de** Lima es mejor que el **de** Cartagena*

Preposition *de* also indicates the day of a month, or the month of a year:

*I was born on the 12th of December 1991 – Nací el 12 **de** diciembre **de** 1991*

Finally, *de* also expresses a type or kind of something:

*I would like to do travel journalism – Me gustaría hacer periodismo **de** viajes*

*I have a typewriter – Tengo una máquina **de** escribir*

*I write for a tourism magazine – Escribo para una revista **de** turismo*

En (at, in, on)

Preposition *en* is normally used to indicate a place or a moment in time:

*I currently live in Spain – Actualmente vivo **en** España*

*I live in Spain, in Palma de Mallorca – Vivo **en** España, **en** Palma de Mallorca*

*I currently work on boats and cruises – Actualmente trabajo **en** barcos y cruceros*

*I spend most of my time at the sea! – ¡Paso casi todo mi tiempo **en** el mar!*

*I took a Spanish course in university – Tomé un curso **en** la universidad*

You can also use this preposition to indicate time:

*I was born in 1993 – Nací **en** el 1993.*

En is also used to indicate languages:

*I'm learning to write in Spanish – Estoy aprendiendo a escribir **en** español*

*I generally write in English – Generalmente escribo **en** inglés*

Para (*for*, *to*)

The preposition *para* indicates an objective, a goal:

*I studied to be a chef – Estudié **para** ser chef*

Con (*with*)

*I'd love to do an internship at a Michelin-star restaurant – Me gustaría hacer una pasantía **en** un restaurante **con** estrellas Michelin.*

A (*to*)

You can use the preposition *a* to indicate someone you are addressing:

*Hello, everyone – Hola **a** todos*

Also, *a* is used to indicate a place you are going to:

*I'll go to Argentina – Iré **a** Argentina*

You can use the preposition *a* to introduce a verb after another verb, as in the following examples:

*I'm learning to write in Spanish – Estoy aprendiendo **a** escribir en español*

*I started to learn Spanish two years ago – Empecé **a** aprender español hace dos años*

Sobre (*about*, *above*, *on*, *over*, *on top of*)

Just like in English, you can use *sobre* (*about*) to introduce a subject:

I write about everything I see – Escribo **sobre** todo lo que veo

But this preposition also means *above, on* or *over*:

The book is on the table – El libro está **sobre** la mesa

Por (*because of, for, around*)

Por indicates cause or reason, as in the following examples:

Because of that, I think it's very important that I learn how to speak Spanish well – **Por** eso, creo que es muy importante que aprenda español muy bien.

But it can be also used as *around* when you are talking about space:

I am traveling around South America – Estoy viajando **por** Sudamérica

Desde (*since*)

Desde indicates origin, especially when talking about time:

I have been traveling for two months – Estoy viajando **desde** hace dos meses

Hasta (*until*):

Hasta is used to talk about a destination or a stop point:

Until now, every person I've met has been great with me – **Hasta** ahora, todas las personas que he conocido han sido geniales conmigo

Contractions (*contracciones*)

There are two contractions in Spanish. When the definite article *el* comes after the prepositions *a* (*to*) or *de* (*from*), they combine to form the contractions *al* and *del*. Examples:

I went **to the** market – Fui **al** mercado

I come **from the** market – Vengo **del** mercado

The only exception is when the article is part of a name (you can tell because it will be capitalized):

I will travel **to El** Paso – Voy a viajar **a El** Paso

Juan is **from El** Salvador – Juan es **de El** Salvador

Lesson 26

Don't Tell Me What To Do!: Imperative Mode

The Spanish imperative mood is used to give orders. There are no tenses in the imperative mood, but there is an affirmative and a negative form. It is not used with all pronouns since you cannot give orders to yourself or to people who are not there.

As you can see, for the *usted, nosotros,* and *ustedes* forms, the imperative is formed using the forms of the present subjunctive, which was explained in the previous chapter.

Regular verbs

To love (*amar*)

tú am**a** / vos am**á** / usted am**e**

nosotros am**emos**

ustedes am**en** / vosotros am**ad**

To fear (*temer*)

tú tem**e** / vos tem**é** / usted tem**a**

nosotros tem**amos**

ustedes tem**an** / vosotros tem**ed**

<u>To live (*vivir*)</u>

tú viv**e** / vos viv**í** / usted viv**a**

nosotros viv**amos**

ustedes viv**an** / vosotros viv**id**

Irregular verbs

<u>To be (*ser*)</u>

tú **sé** / vos **sé** / usted **sea**

nosotros **seamos**

ustedes **sean** / vosotros **sed**

<u>To be (*estar*)</u>

tú **está** / vos **está** / usted **esté**

nosotros **estemos**

ustedes **estén** / vosotros **estad**

<u>To have (*tener*)</u>

tú **ten** / vos **tené** / usted **tenga**

nosotros **tengamos**

ustedes **tengan** / vosotros **tened**

<u>To say (*decir*)</u>

tú **di** / vos **decí** / usted **diga**

nosotros **digamos**

ustedes **digan** / vosotros **decid**

<u>To go (*ir*)</u>

tú **ve** / vos **andá** / usted **vaya**

nosotros **vayamos**

ustedes **vayan** / vosotros **id**

To do (*hacer*)

tú **haz** / vos **hacé** / usted **haga**

nosotros **hagamos**

ustedes **hagan** / vosotros **haced**

To give (*dar*)

tú **da** / vos **da** / usted **dé**

nosotros **demos**

ustedes **den** / vosotros **dad**

Imperative + pronouns

It is very common that object pronouns are attached to the imperative verb:

Tell me what you want to do – **Dime** qué quieres hacer

Tell us more about your family – **Cuéntanos** más sobre tu familia

Buy him something to eat – **Cómprale** algo para comer

Sometimes you can even attach two pronouns, an indirect object, and a direct object pronoun (always in that order):

Tell it to us – Dínoslo

Bring it to me – Tráemelo

Buy it for you – Cómpratelo

Negative commands

Orders not to do something are formed with the adverb "no" + present subjunctive, which was explained in the previous chapter:

Do not look at me – No me mires

Let's not buy more bread – No compremos más pan

Do not tell me what to do – No me digas qué hacer

Lesson 27

Using Adjectives To Tell Your Story

To introduce you to adjectives, let's now look at Andrea's (the hostel's owner) story.

Andrea's story:

Mi nombre es Andrea Del Valle. Soy <u>colombiana,</u> y tengo 38 años, aunque parezco más <u>joven</u> porque siempre estoy rodeada de gente <u>joven</u>.

My name is Andrea Del Valle. I am Colombian, and I am 38 years old, but I look younger because I'm always surrounded by young people.

Crecí en Medellín, pero actualmente vivo en la <u>hermosa</u> Cartagena, donde soy dueña de un <u>pequeño</u> hostal. Me gusta mucho mi trabajo, aunque a veces es un poco <u>estresante</u>.

I grew up in Medellin, but I currently live in beautiful Cartagena, where I own a little hostel. I like my job a lot, though sometimes it can be a bit stressful.

Mi familia era muy <u>pobre</u>, por lo que debí trabajar muchos años para ahorrar el dinero <u>suficiente</u> para tener este negocio.

My family was very poor, so I had to work many years to save enough money to have this business.

Mi padre era carpintero. Mi madre es cocinera: trabaja en un restaurante muy <u>bueno</u> en Medellín. También tengo dos hermanos: un hermano mayor y una hermana menor. Yo nací entre ambos, ¡en el medio!

My father was a carpenter. My mother is a cook: she works at a very good restaurant in Medellin. I also have two siblings: an older brother and a younger sister. I was born between them, in the middle!

También tengo una pareja y dos hijos. Mi pareja se llama Amalia. Nuestros hijos son Javier, de cinco años, y Manuela, de dos años. También tenemos cuatro gatos: ¡somos una <u>gran</u> familia!

I also have a partner and two children. My partner's name is Amalia. Our kids are Javier, who is five years old, and Manuela, who is two years old. We also have four cats: we are a big family!

El año próximo planeo abrir un <u>nuevo</u> alojamiento aquí en Cartagena. No un hostal, sino algo para familias como la nuestra.

Next year I am planning on opening a new hotel, here in Cartagena. Not a hostel, but something for families like ours.

¿Qué más puedo contar sobre mí? La comida que más me gusta es la bandeja paisa, mi color preferido es el <u>azul</u> (como el mar), y me gusta mucho bailar.

What else can I say about me? My favorite food is bandeja paisa, my favorite color is blue (like the sea), and I love dancing.

While in English they normally go before, in Spanish, adjectives are normally put after the noun or pronoun they affect. Another difference is that, in Spanish, adjectives must match gender (feminine or masculine) when possible and quantity (singular or plural).

The **beautiful** car – El automóvil **bello**

The **ugly** house – La casa **fea**

The **fat** cats – Los gatos **gordos**

My **pretty** cousins – Mis primas **bonitas**

In some cases, the adjective can be used before the noun. When you use the adjectives *bueno* (*good*), *malo* (*bad*), and *grande* (*big*), they lose the last letter if you put them before the noun:

A **good** year – Un año **bueno** / Un **buen** año

A **bad** day – Un día **malo** / Un **mal** día

A **big** tree – Un árbol **grande** / Un **gran** árbol

Andrea has many adjectives in her story.

First of all, she says she is Colombian. This is a specific type of adjective, called *adjetivo gentilicio*. These kinds of adjectives indicate the place of origin of a person or an object. You already learned some of these.

Let's see some other adjectives she mentioned and their opposites:

young – joven

old – viejo / vieja

beautiful – hermoso / hermosa

ugly – feo / fea

small – pequeño / pequeña

big – grande

stressful – estresante

relaxing – relajante

poor – pobre

rich – rico / rica

enough – suficiente

good – bueno / buena

bad – malo / mala

new – nuevo / nueva

old – viejo / vieja

Let's see some more sentences with these common adjectives:

This country is really young – Este país es muy joven

María's car is very old – El auto de María es muy viejo

Your city is beautiful – Tu ciudad es hermosa

To me, pigeons are ugly – Para mí, las palomas son feas

Beds are too small – Las camas son demasiado pequeñas

Give me the biggest coffee you have – Dame el café más grande que tengas

My job is stressful – Mi trabajo es estresante

I need relaxing holidays – Necesito unas vacaciones relajantes

My grandparents were really poor – Mis abuelos eran muy pobres

The president is rich – La presidenta es rica

Three mojitos are enough – Tres mojitos son suficientes

The view is very good – La vista es muy buena

It was a very bad flight, with loads of turbulence – Fue un vuelo muy malo, con muchas turbulencias

I have a new plan – Tengo un nuevo plan

Finally, Andrea said her favorite color was *blue*. Blue and every color is also an adjective. Let's look at other colors in Spanish:

black – negro

white – blanco

gray – gris

red – rojo / colorado

blue – azul

yellow – amarillo

green – verde

orange – naranja / anaranjado

purple – violeta / morado / púrpura

brown – marrón / café

Let's see some practical examples with colors so that you can paint a whole rainbow with your vocabulary:

Tonight I'm wearing a black dress – Esta noche llevaré un vestido negro

He is beautiful; he has a lovely white smile – Es hermoso; tiene una sonrisa blanca adorable

The sky is gray; we should not go out – El cielo está gris; no deberíamos salir

What is the name of those red birds? – ¿Cómo es el nombre de esas aves coloradas?

I never saw such a blue ocean – Nunca vi un océano tan azul

Do you feel fine? You look... yellow – ¿Te sientes bien? Te ves... amarillo

The region is so green this time of the year! – ¡La región es tan verde en esta época del año!

We use orange clothes so they can find us if we get lost in the mountains – Usamos ropa naranja para que nos encuentren si nos perdemos en la montaña

I fell on the ground, and my knees are purple now – Me caí en el piso, y ahora mis rodillas están moradas

After today's hike, my new white shoes are brown – Después de la caminata de hoy, mis nuevas zapatillas blancas ya son marrones

Lesson 28

You Need What?: Subjunctive Mode

The Spanish subjunctive is used to talk about desires, doubts, the unknown, the abstract, and some emotions. The subjunctive includes many of the same tenses as the indicative, but in this chapter, you are only going to learn the present subjunctive tense and a past subjunctive tense used in conditional sentences.

For English speakers, sometimes the subjunctive can be difficult to understand, but with practice, you will get it. To start, try to remember the following situations where you have to use it:

1. Sentences with two subjects: sentences with one subject in the main clause and one in the noun clause use the subjunctive.

2. Sentences linked with a relative pronoun: sentences that have parts linked by a relative pronoun (que, quien, como).

3. Sentences that have two verbs, and the first one expresses wishes, emotions, impersonal expressions, recommendations, doubt, and denial.

Examples:

I need you to **do** something for me – Necesito que **hagas** algo por mí

He wants me to **buy** him the new videogame console – Él quiere que le **compre** la nueva consola de videojuegos

They expect us to **solve** everything – Ellos esperan que nosotros **resolvamos** todo

I doubt he **can** make it – Dudo que él **pueda** hacerlo

I want us to **go** on a trip – Quiero que nos **vayamos** de viaje

She refuses to believe he **is** guilty – Se niega a creer que él **sea** el culpable

We hope you **are** the architect we need – Esperamos que **seas** el arquitecto que necesitamos

I hate that you **talk** to me like that – Odio que me **hables** así

I am glad that you **love** each other again – Me alegra que se **amen** nuevamente

It is necessary that someone **fixes** it – Es necesario que alguien lo **arregle**

He recommended that I **exercise** more – Me recomendó que me **ejercite** más

I wish the food **tastes** as good as it looks – Ojalá la comida **sepa** tan bien como se ve

I wish my son **passes** his driving test – Ojalá mi hijo **apruebe** su examen de conducir

Present subjunctive (*presente del subjuntivo*)

To love (*amar*)

que yo am**e**

que tú am**es** / vos am**es** / usted am**e**

que él/ella am**e**

que nosotros am**emos**

que ustedes am**en** / vosotros am**éis**

que ellos/ellas am**en**

To fear (*temer*)

que yo tem**a**

que tú tem**as** / vos tem**as** / usted tem**a**

que él/ella tem**a**

que nosotros tem**amos**

que ustedes tem**an** / vosotros tem**áis**

que ellos/ellas tem**an**

To live (*vivir*)

que yo viv**a**

que tú viv**as** / vos viv**as** / usted viv**a**

que él/ella viv**a**

que nosotros viv**amos**

que ustedes viv**an** / vosotros viv**áis**

que ellos/ellas viv**an**

To be (*ser*)

que yo **sea**

que tú **seas** / vos **seas** / usted **sea**

que él/ella **sea**

que nosotros **seamos**

que ustedes **sean** / vosotros **seáis**

que ellos/ellas **sean**

To be (*estar*)

que yo **esté**

que tú **estés** / vos **estés** / usted **esté**

que él/ella **esté**

que nosotros **estemos**

que ustedes **estén** / vosotros **estéis**

que ellos/ellas **estén**

<u>To have (*tener*)</u>

que yo **tenga**

que tú **tengas** / vos **tengas** / usted **tenga**

que él/ella **tenga**

que nosotros **tengamos**

que ustedes **tengan** / vosotros **tengáis**

que ellos/ellas **tengan**

<u>To say (*decir*)</u>

que yo **diga**

que tú **digas** / vos **digas** / usted **diga**

que él/ella **diga**

que nosotros **digamos**

que ustedes **digan** / vosotros **digáis**

que ellos/ellas **digan**

<u>To go (*ir*)</u>

que yo **vaya**

que tú **vayas** / vos **vayas** / usted **vaya**

que él/ella **vaya**

que nosotros **vayamos**

que ustedes **vayan** / vosotros **vayáis**

que ellos/ellas **vayan**

To do (*hacer*)

que yo **haga**

que tú **hagas** / vos **hagas** / usted **haga**

que él/ella **haga**

que nosotros **hagamos**

que ustedes **hagan** / vosotros **hagáis**

que ellos/ellas **hagan**

Can (*poder*)

que yo **pueda**

que tú **puedas** / vos **puedas** / usted **pueda**

que él/ella **pueda**

que nosotros **podamos**

que ustedes **puedan** / vosotros **podáis**

que ellos/ellas **puedan**

To see (*ver*)

que yo **vea**

que tú **veas** / vos **veas** / usted **vea**

que él/ella **vea**

que nosotros **veamos**

que ustedes **vean** / vosotros **veáis**

que ellos/ellas **vean**

To give (*dar*)

que yo **dé**

que tú **des** / vos **des** / usted **dé**

que él/ella **dé**

que nosotros **demos**

que ustedes **den** / vosotros **deis**

que ellos/ellas **den**

To want (*querer*)

que yo **quiera**

que tú **quieras** / vos **quieras** / usted **quiera**

que él/ella **quiera**

que nosotros **queramos**

que ustedes **quieran** / vosotros **queráis**

que ellos/ellas **quieran**

Here are some sentences with the subjunctive mode:

The audience wants you to sing a love song – El público quiere que **cantes** *una serenata*

We will be more relaxed when we earn a good salary – Estaremos más tranquilos cuando **ganemos** *un buen sueldo*

You can't force him to love you – No puedes obligarlo a que te **ame**

I hope the dog does not break his new toy – Espero que el perro no **rompa** *su juguete nuevo*

My grandparents want us to live with them for some time – Mis abuelos quieren que **vivamos** *con ellos por un tiempo*

It doesn't matter how hard I study, my parents will never be happy – No importa cuánto **estudie**, *mis padres nunca estarán satisfechos*

My wife wants our daughter to be a doctor – Mi esposa quiere que nuestra hija **sea** *médica*

My mother always makes sure we are happy – Mi mamá se asegura de que siempre **estemos** *felices*

The day I'm the boss, things will change – El día que **sea** *el jefe, las cosas cambiarán*

*I can't get Juan to be relaxed – No logro que Juan **esté** tranquilo*

*I want a house with three bedrooms – Quiero una casa que **tenga** tres habitaciones*

*I need someone to tell me the truth – Necesito alguien que me **diga** la verdad*

*My cousins want us to go visit – Mis primos quieren que **vayamos** de visita*

*I need a masseuse who makes miracles – Necesito una masajista que **haga** milagros*

*When you can, let's get together to study – Cuando **podáis**, juntémonos para estudiar*

*When you see where the problem is, we will be able to fix it – Cuando **veas** dónde está el problema, podremos solucionarlo*

*We need someone to give us directions – Necesitamos a alguien que nos **dé** indicaciones*

*We haven't met anyone who wants to travel with us – No conocimos a nadie que **quiera** viajar con nosotros*

*Tell Jorge to go shopping – Dile a Jorge que **vaya** a hacer las compras*

Lesson 29

Using Adverbs To Tell Your Story

Just as adjectives modify nouns, adverbs modify verbs. They normally answer these questions: "how?", "how much?", "when?" and "where?" Luckily, adverbs do not have to match number and gender, which means they are *invariable*. This makes them much easier to use. Just as in English, adverbs are normally placed *after* the verb they modify:

*You speak **slowly** – Habláis **lentamente***

*I like you **a lot** – Me gustas **mucho***

*He complains **constantly** – Se queja **constantemente***

Kate and James had a lovely week in Peru, and now they have moved on to Chile. Like any two siblings, after more than a week traveling together, they start to quarrell a bit:

*KATE: Can you walk faster? You are too slow! – ¿Puedes caminar más **rápidamente**? Eres muy lento*

*JAMES: Why do you complain constantly? Don't you have anything better to do? – ¿Por qué te quejas **constantemente**? ¿No tienes nada mejor que hacer?*

*KATE: I would complain less if you did not walk so slowly – Me quejaría menos si no caminaras tan **lentamente***

*JAMES: We are fighting a lot lately – Estamos peleando mucho **últimamente***

*KATE: I know. Apparently, it is what we do when we know we do not have a lot of time together left – Lo sé. **Aparentemente**, es lo que hacemos cuando sabemos que no nos queda mucho tiempo juntos*

JAME: Oh, I will miss you too – Oh, yo también te voy a extrañar

Adverbs of place

These adverbs answer *where* something happens. The most common adverbs of place are the following:

in front of – adelante/delante

on top of – arriba/encima

behind – atrás/detrás

there – ahí/allí/allá

here – aquí/acá

near – cerca

far – lejos

where – donde/adonde

Here are these adverbs in practical sentences:

*The truth is in front of you – La verdad está **delante** tuyo*

*I left the tickets on top of the fridge – Dejé las entradas **encima** del refrigerador*

*He is probably hiding behind the door – Probablemente está ocultándose **detrás** de la puerta*

*I always wanted to travel there – Siempre quise viajar **allí***

*We are here for you – Estamos **acá** para vos*

*I want to buy a house near my workplace – Quiero comprar una casa **cerca** de mi lugar de trabajo*

*Do not go too far! –– ¡No vayas demasiado **lejos**!*

*It should be where I left it – Debería estar **donde** lo dejé*

Adverbs of time

These adverbs answer *when, for how long* or *how often* something happens. The most common adverbs of time are the following:

before – antes

after – después

later – luego

soon – pronto/próximamente

late – tarde

early – temprano

still – todavía/aún

yet – aún

now – ya/ahora

yesterday – ayer

today – hoy

tomorrow – mañana

always – siempre

never – nunca/jamás

last night – anoche

right away – enseguida

while – mientras

Let's use these adverbs in some real-life sentences:

*Call me before you come – Llámame **antes** de venir*

We can meet after class – Podemos vernos **después** de clases

See you later! – ¡Nos vemos **luego**!

We will find out **soon** – Lo descubriremos **pronto**

She is always **late** – Ella siempre llega **tarde**

I want to be there early – Quiero estar allí **temprano**

I am still in love with him – **Todavía** estoy enamorado de él

They have not arrived yet – No han llegado **aún**

I want to know your answer now – Quiero saber tu respuesta **ahora**

I saw it yesterday – Lo vi **ayer**

Can we do it today? – ¿Podemos hacerlo **hoy**?

We are hiking tomorrow – **Mañana** nos vamos de excursión

I will always remember this journey – **Siempre** recordaré este viaje

I never went there – **Nunca** fui allí

We had an amazing party last night – Hicimos una fiesta increíble **anoche**

I will be there right away – Estaré allí **enseguida**

I thought a lot while walking – Pensé mucho **mientras** caminaba

Adverbs of quantity

These adverbs answer the question *how much*. The most common adverbs of quantity are the following:

very – muy

little – poco

a lot – mucho

pretty – bastante

more – más

less – menos

some – algo

too much – demasiado

almost – casi

only – solo/solamente

so – tan

so much – tanto

everything – todo

nothing – nada

approximately – aproximadamente

Let's use these words in sentences:

*I am very tired – Estoy **muy** cansada*

*I have little time – Tengo **poco** tiempo*

*I love you a lot – Te quiero **mucho***

*I am pretty anxious – Estoy **bastante** ansioso*

*We want more – Queremos **más***

*They gave me less than last time – Me dieron **menos** que la vez anterior*

*I have some experience – Tengo **algo** de experiencia*

*We ordered too much – Pedimos **demasiado***

*We are almost there! – ¡Ya **casi** llegamos!*

*We should take only what is necessary – Deberíamos llevar **solamente** lo necesario*

*We are so lazy! – ¡Somos **tan** perezosos!*

*I have so much to give – Tengo **tanto** para dar*

*I want to see everything – Quiero ver **todo***

Nothing could make me sad now – **Nada** *podría ponerme triste ahora*

We need approximately one kilo of flour – *Necesitamos* **aproximadamente** *un kilo de harina*

Adverbs of manner

As you saw at the beginning of this lesson, the adverbs of manner are normally formed by adding the suffix *-mente* to an adjective. In English, the same happens with the suffix *-ly*. Adverbs that end in *-mente* (*-ly*) keep the accentuation of the original word, as if the *-mente* suffix were not there, even though they are always stressed in the second to last syllable:

easy, easily – fácil, fácilmente

responsible, responsively – responsable, responsablemente

careless, carelessly – descuidado, descuidadamente

clear, clearly – claro, claramente

quick, quickly – veloz, velozmente

But, of course, there are exceptions! Here are some adverbs of manner that do not end in *-mente*:

well – bien

bad – mal

regular – regular

slowly – despacio

fast – deprisa/aprisa

like that – así

as – como

on purpose – adrede

worse – peor

better – mejor

Let's see some examples of all of these:

*He does everything easily – Hace todo **fácilmente***

*We must solve this responsively – Debemos resolver esto **responsablemente***

I am tired of things done carelessly – Estoy cansada de que las cosas se hagan descuidadamente

*Say it clearly – Dilo **claramente***

*Come quickly! – ¡Ven **velozmente**!*

*I feel well – Me siento **bien***

*I feel bad – Me siento **mal***

*He is always regular – Es siempre **regular***

*Transport moves quite slowly – El transporte va bastante **despacio***

*We are too fast for them – Vamos demasiado **aprisa** para ellos*

*I do not like things like that – No me gustan las cosas **así***

*I am happy as a baby – Estoy feliz **como** un bebé*

*They did it on purpose – Lo han hecho **adrede***

*It is worse than our first option – Es **peor** que nuestra primera opción*

*I feel much better – Me siento mucho **mejor***

Lesson 30

The Best Part of Traveling: Food and Drink

Tasting different foods and trying the local cuisine is certainly one of the best parts of visiting a foreign country. Before you sit down at a local restaurant before a big meal, you should, of course, take some time to find out how to talk to the waiter or waitress or how to order your dish. Many restaurants offer menus with a translation, but if you also want to move beyond the tourist trails, you may have to come to terms with a menu in Spanish!

Let's see some basic sentences, with some verbs you already know (*pedir, estar, gustar, hacer*):

Can I please order this dish – ¿Puedo pedir este plato, por favor?

It is delicious! – ¡Está delicioso!

I would like another portion of tortilla – Me gustaría otra porción de tortilla

What's the best wine to go with this dish? – ¿Cuál es el mejor vino para beber con este plato?

What's the recipe? – ¿Cuál es la receta?

Thank you for a wonderful meal! – ¡Gracias por una deliciosa comida!

Food vocabulary

table – mesa

menu – menú

kitchen – cocina

vegetarian – vegetariano/a

I do not eat pork – No como cerdo

I do not eat beef – No como carne de vaca

I only eat kosher food – Solo como comida kosher

breakfast – desayuno

lunch – almuerzo

dinner – cena

dessert – postre

chicken – pollo

beef – res / carne de vaca

fish – pescado

ham – jamón

sausages – salchichas

cheese – queso

eggs – huevos

salad – ensalada

vegetables – vegetales

fruit – fruta

bread – pan

toast – tostadas

pasta – pasta

rice – arroz

beans – frijoles

potatoes – papas

May I have a glass of...? – ¿Puedo tomar un vaso / una copa de...?

May I have a bottle of...? – ¿Puedo tomar una botella de...?

coffee – café

tea – té

juice – jugo/zumo

water – agua

beer – cerveza

red/white wine – vino tinto/blanco

salt – sal

black pepper – pimienta

butter – manteca

Excuse me, waiter? – ¿Disculpe, mesero/camarero/mozo?

It was delicious – Estaba delicioso

The check, please – La cuenta, por favor

food – comida

tip – propina

Reservation and ordering

Una mesa para uno/dos, por favor – A table for one person/two people, please

¿Puedo ver el menú, por favor? – Can I look at the menu, please?

¿Puedo ver la cocina? – Can I look in the kitchen?

¿Hay una especialidad de la casa? – Is there a house specialty?

¿Hay una especialidad local? – Is there a local specialty?

Soy vegetariano/a – I'm a vegetarian

No como cerdo – I don't eat pork

No como carne de vaca – I don't eat beef

Solo como comida kosher – I only eat kosher food

a la carta – a la carte

desayuno – breakfast

almuerzo – lunch

merienda – teatime

cena – dinner

Me gustaría… – I would like…

Quiero un platillo que tenga… – I want a dish containing…

pollo – chicken

res – beef

pescado – fish

jamón – ham

salchichas – sausages

queso – cheese

huevos – eggs

ensalada – salad

vegetales – vegetables

fruta – fruit

pan – bread

tostadas – toast

fideos – noodles

pasta – pasta

arroz – rice

frijoles – beans

papas – potatoes

¿Puedo tomar un vaso de…? – May I have a glass of…?

¿Puedo tomar una copa de…? – May I have a cup of…?

¿Puedo tomar una botella de…? – May I have a bottle of…?

café – coffee

té – tea

jugo/zumo – juice

agua – water

cerveza – beer

vino tinto/blanco – red/white wine

¿Podría darme…? – May I have some…?

sal – salt

pimienta – black pepper

manteca – butter

¿Disculpe, mesero/camarero/mozo? – Excuse me, waiter?

He terminado – I'm finished

Estaba delicioso – It was delicious

Por favor, levante los platos – Please, clear the plates

La cuenta, por favor – The check, please

Ordering snacks

¿Tiene bocadillos? – Do you have any snacks?

¿Tiene sándwiches? – Do you have any sandwiches?

¿Sirven comida? – Do you serve food?

¿A qué hora cierra la cocina? – What time does the kitchen close?

¿Aún se sirve comida aquí? – Are you still serving food?

Unas patatas fritas de paquete, por favor – A packet of crisps, please

¿Qué sabor le gustaría? – What flavor would you like?

saladas – salted

queso y cebolla – cheese and onion

sal y vinagre – salt and vinegar

¿Qué tipo de sándwiches tienen? – What sort of sandwiches do you have?

¿Tienen platos calientes? – Do you have any hot food?

Los especiales del día están en la pizarra – Today's specials are on the board

¿Es servicio a la carta o autoservicio? – Is it table service or self-service?

¿Qué le puedo traer? – What can I get you?

¿Quiere algo de comer? – Would you like anything to eat?

¿Puedo ver un menú, por favor? – Could we see a menu, please?

¿Para llevar o para comer aquí? – Eat in or take away?

Food-related terms

fresco – fresh

viejo – moldy

podrido – rotten

jugoso – juicy

---

maduro – ripe

verde – unripe

tierno – tender

duro – tough

quemado – burnt

pasado – overcooked

crudo – underdone/raw

bien cocido – well done

delicioso – delicious

horrible – horrible

salado – salty

salado – savory

dulce – sweet

agrio – sour

sabroso – tasty

picante – spicy/hot

suave – mild

hornear – to bake

hervir – to boil

freir – to fry

grillar – to grill

rostizar – to roast

cocinar al vapor – to steam

desayuno – breakfast

almuerzo – lunch

merienda – teatime

cena – dinner

desayunar – to have breakfast

almorzar – to have lunch

cenar – to have dinner

ingrediente – ingredient

receta – recipe

cocinar – to cook

poner la mesa – to set the table

levantar/recoger la mesa – to clear the table

sentarse a la mesa – to come to the table

limpiar la mesa – to wipe the table

preparar una comida – to prepare a meal

el bar – the bar

cocinero/chef – cook/chef

reserva – reservation

menú – menu

mesero/camarero/mozo – waiter

mesera/camarera/moza – waitress

carta de vinos – wine list

entrante/entrada/aperitivo – starter

plato principal – main course

postre – dessert

servicio – service

cobro de servicio – service charge

Drinks

jugo/zumo de frutas – fruit juice

jugo/zumo de naranja – orange juice

té helado – iced tea

limonada – lemonade

batido – milkshake

agua – water

agua mineral – mineral water

agua con gas – sparkling water

agua del grifo – tap water

chocolatada – cocoa

café – coffee

café negro – black coffee

café descafeinado – decaffeinated coffee

té verde – green tea

té de hierbas – herbal tea

chocolate caliente – hot chocolate

té – tea

saquito de té – tea bag

fuerte – strong

cerveza – beer

vino – wine

vino tinto – red wine

vino blanco – white wine

vino rosado – rosé

vino espumante – sparkling wine

champaña – champagne

licor – liqueur

ron – rum

whisky – whiskey

vodka – vodka

alcohol – alcohol

bar – bar

tabernero/camarero/barman – barman

vaso de cerveza – beer glass

botella – bottle

lata – can

cócktail – cocktail

borracho/ebrio – drunk

resaca – hangover

sobrio – sober

bebidas blancas – spirits

copa de vino – wine glass

Ordering at the bar

¿Se sirve alcohol? – Do you serve alcohol?

¿Hay servicio de mesa? – Is there table service?

Una cerveza/dos cervezas, por favor – A beer/two beers, please

Un vaso de vino tinto/blanco, por favor – A glass of red/white wine, please

Un vaso, por favor – A glass, please

Una pinta, por favor – *A pint, please*

Una botella, por favor – *A bottle, please*

¿Tiene bocadillos? – *Do you have any bar snacks?*

Uno más, por favor – *One more, please*

Otra ronda, por favor – *Another round, please*

¿Cuándo cierra el bar? – *When is closing time?*

¿Qué le gustaría beber? – *What would you like to drink?*

¿Qué va a pedir? – *What are you having?*

¿Qué le puedo traer? – *What can I get you?*

Voy a querer..., por favor – *I'll have..., please*

una pinta de cerveza – *a pint of lager*

una copa de vino blanco – *a glass of white wine*

una copa de vino tinto – *a glass of red wine*

un jugo de naranja – *an orange juice*

un café – *a coffee*

una cola/una Coca Cola – *a Coke*

una Coca Cola Light – *a Diet Coke*

¿Grande o pequeño/a? – *Large or small?*

¿Lo quiere con hielo? – *Would you like ice with that?*

Sin hielo, por favor – *No ice, please*

Un poco, por favor – *A little, please*

Mucho hielo, por favor – *Lots of ice, please*

Una cerveza, por favor – *A beer, please*

Dos cervezas, por favor – *Two beers, please*

Tres chupitos de tequila, por favor – *Three shots of tequila, please*

¿Ya está atendido? – Are you already being served?

Estamos atendidos, gracias – We're being served, thanks

¿Quién sigue? – Who's next?

¿Qué vino le gustaría? – Which wine would you like?

El vino de la casa está bien – House wine is fine

¿Qué cerveza le gustaría? – Which beer would you like?

¿Le gustaría cerveza tirada o en botella? – Would you like draught or bottled beer?

Lo mismo para mí, por favor – I'll have the same, please

Nada para mí, gracias – Nothing for me, thanks

Quiero esto – I'll get this

¡Quédese con el cambio! – Keep the change!

¡Salud! – Cheers!

¿A quién le toca pagar la ronda? – Whose round is it?

Me toca pagar la ronda – It's my round

Te toca pagar la ronda – It's your round

Otra cerveza, por favor – Another beer, please

Dos cervezas más, por favor – Another two beers, please

Lo mismo otra vez, por favor – Same again, please

¿Aún sirven bebidas? – Are you still serving drinks?

¡Última ronda! – Last orders!

Lesson 31
Less is More: Objects and Things

For some reason, every Spanish noun has a gender, even if it is an object or an abstract concept. This means articles and adjectives must match their gender too. Normally, masculine nouns end in *o* and feminine nouns end in *a*.

In English, there is one definite article: *the*. In Spanish, however, there is one for masculine words and one for feminine words. These are *el* and *la*.

Note that the masculine article *el* is differentiated from the personal pronoun *él* with a *tilde*, even though both words are normally pronounced in the same way (sometimes *él* is stressed harder).

Here are some masculine nouns ending in *o*:

the phone – el teléfono

the game – el juego

the pen – el bolígrafo

the road – el camino

the notebook – el cuaderno

the book – el libro

the shoe – el zapato

Let's use them in some sentences:

*Do you have James' phone – ¿Tienes **el teléfono** de James?*

*I won the game! – ¡Gané **el juego**!*

*Where is the pen? – ¿Dónde está **el bolígrafo**?*

*Watch the road while you drive – Mira **el camino** mientras conduces*

*The notebook is the only tool I need – **El cuaderno** es la única herramienta que necesito*

*Have you read the book by Patricio Pron? – ¿Has leído **el libro** de Patricio Pron?*

*The shoe broke during the hike – **El zapato** se rompió durante la excursión*

And here are some feminine nouns ending in *a*:

the door – la puerta

the chair – la silla

the kitchen – la cocina

the party – la fiesta

the moon – la luna

the table – la mesa

the nose – la nariz

Let's use these in some sentences:

*Close the door, please – Cierra **la puerta**, por favor*

*Can I take the chair? – ¿Puedo tomar **la silla**?*

*There is a big surprise for you in the kitchen – Hay una gran sorpresa para vosotras en **la cocina***

*The party will be an absolute success – **La fiesta** será un enorme éxito*

*Look at the moon! It is beautiful! – ¡Mira **la luna**! ¡Es hermosa!*

*We all don't fit at the table – No entramos todos en **la mesa***

*You have the most beautiful nose I have seen – Tienes **la nariz** más bella que he visto*

However, there are exceptions. And feminine and masculine nouns that end in other letters, or even masculine nouns that end in *a* and feminine nouns that end in *o*, but, luckily for you, they are not so common:

Here are masculine nouns that do not end in *o:*

the paper – el papel

the tree – el árbol

the bread – el pan

the coffee – el café

love – el amor

Monday – el lunes

the problem – el problema

the weather – el clima

Here are feminine nouns that do not end in *a:*

the night – la noche

the skin – la piel

the class – la clase

the snow – la nieve

the picture – la foto

the hand – la mano

the image – la imagen

the people – la gente

Let's use all of these in real-life sentences:

*Throw the paper into the bin – Tira **el papel** al cesto*

*The kids climb the tree – Los niños trepan **el árbol***

*Even the bread is getting expensive here – Incluso **el pan** se está poniendo caro aquí*

*The coffee in Colombia is incomparable – **El café** en Colombia es incomparable*

*I think she is the love of my life – Creo que ella es **el amor** de mi vida*

*On Monday I am leaving – **El lunes** me voy*

*The problem is we live in different countries – **El problema** es que vivimos en países diferentes*

*The weather is just perfect here – **El clima** es simplemente perfecto aquí*

*You looked beautiful on the night we met – Te veías hermosa **la noche** en que nos conocimos*

*Your skin is very red – Tienes **la piel** muy colorada*

*The class was very good; I learned many nouns – **La clase** estuvo muy bien; aprendí muchos sustantivos*

*The snow is white when it's clean – **La nieve** es blanca cuando está limpia*

*Just take the picture! I am tired of smiling – ¡Ya toma **la foto**! Estoy cansado de sonreír*

*Give me your hand; I do not want to fall – Dame **la mano**; no quiero caerme*

*I will never forget the image of this sunrise at the beach – Nunca olvidaré **la imagen** de este amanecer en la playa*

*People are crazy, always, everywhere – **La gente** está loca, siempre, en todos lados*

Some feminine words use the masculine article *el* when they start with a stressed *a*. Even if they use the masculine article, they are still feminine words, which means the adjectives that affect them must be feminine:

the clear water – el agua clara

the bald eagle – el águila calva

the broken wing – el ala rota

the housekeeper – el ama de llaves

There are also plurals for definite articles: *los* and *las*. You have to use these when you talk about more than one noun:

the cats – los gatos

the houses – las casas

the friends – los amigos

the cars – los autos

the whales – las ballenas

the cakes – las tortas

the shoes – los zapatos

Let's use these in some sentences:

*My sister's cats are all crazy – **Los gatos** gatos de mi hermana están todos locos*

*The houses of this city are so pretty! – ¡**Las casas** de esta ciudad son tan hermosas!*

*My brother's friends are coming to Peru – **Los amigos** de mi hermano vendrán a Perú*

*Cars are very old in Cuba – **Los autos** son muy viejos en Cuba*

*You can see the whales in the south of Argentina – Puedes ver **las ballenas** en el sur de Argentina*

*You can also try the Welsh cakes there – También puedes probar **las tortas** galesas allí*

*The shoes are too big for you – **Los zapatos** son demasiado grandes para ti*

Indefinite articles

Just like it was mentioned in Lesson 16, when talking about number *one*, indefinite articles in Spanish are *un* and *una*:

These are the masculine nouns you learned before with their indefinite article:

a phone – un teléfono

a game – un juego

a pen – un bolígrafo

a road – un camino

a notebook – un cuaderno

a book – un libro

a shoe – un zapato

a tree – un árbol

a coffee – un café

a problem – un problema

These are the feminine nouns you learned before with their indefinite article:

a door – una puerta

a chair – una silla

a kitchen – una cocina

a party – una fiesta

a table – una mesa

a night – una noche

a class – una clase

a picture – una foto

a hand – una mano

an image – una imagen

a person – una persona

James is in Argentina. After saying goodbye to his sister, Kate, he took a plane from Santiago de Chile to Buenos Aires. In Buenos Aires, he is staying at a friend's house. He meets his friend, Sara, in London. She lived there for a year, but now she is back in Argentina. On James' first night in Buenos Aires, Sara takes James out for some drinks:

*SARA: What do you think of the bar? – ¿Qué te parece **el bar**?*

*JAMES: It is great! Is every bar so fancy in Buenos Aires? – ¡Es genial! ¿Todos **los bares** son tan elegantes en Buenos Aires?*

*SARA: No, of course not, but after work I like drinking the best cocktails – No, claro que no, pero después **del trabajo** me gusta tomar **los cóctails** más ricos.*

*JAMES: I like the cocktail you ordered me very much – Me gusta mucho **el trago** que me pediste*

*SARA: Hold up the glass; I want to take a picture of you – Sostén **el vaso** en alto; quiero tomarte **una foto***

*JAMES: What is the word you say here when you take a picture? Is it 'cheese'? – ¿Cuál es **la palabra** que dicen aquí cuando se sacan una foto? ¿Es 'queso'?*

SARA: No, it is 'whiskey'! – No, ¡es 'whiskey'!

Lesson 32

This and That: Demonstrative Pronouns

While in English, you have *this* and *that*, in Spanish, there are three demonstrative pronouns: *este, ese* and *aquel*, and their feminine forms and plurals.

Este is used to talk about a noun that is close to the speaker:

this pencil – este lápiz

this mug – esta taza

these objects – estos objetos

these spoons – estas cucharas

Ese is used to talk about something not very close to the speaker (though it may be close to the listener):

that problem – ese problema

that house – esa casa

those years – esos años

those oranges – esas naranjas

Aquel is used to replace something far from both the speaker and the listener:

that day – aquel día

that woman – aquella mujer

those students – aquellos estudiantes

those girls – aquellas niñas

Let's see demonstrative pronouns in some sentences:

This pencil is very sharp – Este lápiz está muy afilado

This mug is mine! – ¡Esta taza es mía!

I want to throw away all of these objects – Quiero botar todos estos objetos

Let's buy these spoons – Compremos estas cucharas

Forget about that problem – Olvida ese problema

She wants to live in that house – Ella quiere vivir en esa casa

I remember those years – Recuerdo esos años

Hand me those oranges – Pásame esas naranjas

Were you there that day? – ¿Estabas allí aquel día?

Who is that woman? – ¿Quién es aquella mujer?

Talk with those students – Habla con aquellos estudiantes

Those girls are my daughters – Aquellas niñas son mis hijas

James has not been himself since he left Cartagena. The truth is he is constantly thinking about Daniela, the Mexican girl he met there. He also misses the city, for sure, but Dani made some impression on him. His friend Sara notices something is going on with him:

*SARA: What is that face? – ¿Qué es **esa** cara?*

*JAMES: What is that question? – ¿Qué es **esa** pregunta?*

*SARA: Come on, James, I know something is going on with you; I know about these things – Vamos, James, sé que te pasa algo; sé sobre **estas** cosas*

*JAMES: Okay, the thing is there is this girl… – Bueno, el tema es que está **esta** chica…*

*SARA: A girl? James is having love problems? I never imagined this! – ¿Una chica? ¿James con problemas de amor? ¡**Esto** nunca me lo imaginé!*

*JAMES: Well, it is not the first time I like someone. That time with Erika? – Bueno, no es la primera vez que me gusta alguien. ¿Y **aquella** vez con Erika?*

*SARA: That was nothing. Now this… this is really troubling you – **Aquello** no fue nada. En cambio **esto**… **Esto** te está molestando.*

*JAMES: Yes, it is true. This time it is stronger – Sí, es cierto. **Esta** vez es más fuerte*

*SARA: Do not worry. This time you have your friend here to give you advice – No te preocupes. **Esta** vez tenés a tu amiga acá para darte consejos*

*JAMES: What should I do? This girl lives in Mexico – ¿Qué debería hacer? **Esta** chica vive en México*

*SARA: And that is a problem because… – ¿Y **eso** es un problema porque…?*

*JAMES: Well, that is right! I can just go there, right? – Bueno, ¡**eso** es verdad! puedo simplemente ir allí, ¿no?*

*SARE: Yes! That is my boy! – ¡Sí! ¡**Ese** es mi amigo!*

Lesson 33

The Curious Traveler: Questions and Answers

If you are going to travel around Latin America or Spain, you are definitely going to be asking loads of questions. Learning a new language is not only learning new words; it is learning about a whole new culture.

This is why you need to be ready to ask, and ask and ask even more, and also get ready to hear some answers!

Have you ever heard of the six *W* and the two *H*? They are *what, when, who, where, why, which, how,* and *how much*? In Spanish, these could be translated as *qué, cuándo, quién, dónde, por qué, cuál, cómo* and *cuánto*.

These words are fundamental if, let's say, you want to buy something (*how much is that?*), if you want to move around (*where is the train station?*) or even if you want to know the time (*what time is it?*).

What? (¿Qué?)

What are you doing here? – ¿Qué estás haciendo aquí?

What are we going to eat? – ¿Qué vamos a comer?

What do you mean? – ¿Qué quieres decir?

What do we do now? – ¿Qué hacemos ahora?

What's up, guys? – ¿Qué pasa, chicos?

What time is it? – ¿Qué hora es?

¿Cuándo?

When is our plane leaving? – ¿Cuándo sale nuestro avión?

When is Sara picking you up? – ¿Cuándo te recoge Sara?

When is your thesis due? – ¿Cuándo debes entregar la tesis?

When are you coming to visit? – ¿Cuándo vienes de visita?

When are we going to Machu Picchu? – ¿Cuándo vamos a Machu Picchu?

When is the bus coming? – ¿Cuándo viene el bus?

¿Quién?

Who was that girl? – ¿Quién era esa chica?

Who do we have to talk to? – ¿Con quién tenemos que hablar?

Who is in charge here? – ¿Quién está a cargo aquí?

Who are you? – ¿Quién eres?

Who do you think you are? – ¿Quién crees que eres?

Who could have imagined something like this? – ¡Quién podría haber imaginado algo así!

¿Dónde?

Where are you? – ¿Dónde estás?

Where is this hotel? – ¿Dónde está este hotel?

Where do you want to go? – ¿Dónde quieres ir?

Where is my phone?! – ¡¿Dónde está mi teléfono?!

Where do we go afterward? – ¿Dónde vamos a continuación?

Where is this place?! – ¿¡Dónde está este sitio!?

¿Por qué?

Why do you want to go there? – ¿Por qué quieres ir ahí?

Why do we have to go there? – ¿Por qué tenemos que ir allí?

Why don't we go back? – ¿Por qué no regresamos?

Why are you running? – ¿Por qué corres?

Why don't we order everything on the menu? – ¿Por qué no pedimos todo lo que hay en el menú?

Why don't we open a bottle of champagne? – ¿Por qué no abrimos una botella de champán?

¿Cómo?

How do we go back to the house? – ¿Cómo volvemos a la casa?

How did we get here? – ¿Cómo llegamos aquí?

How did this happen? – ¿Cómo pasó esto?

How can I return the favor? – ¿Cómo puedo devolverte el favor?

How do you know my name? – ¿Cómo sabes mi nombre?

How can I help you? – ¿Cómo puedo ayudarte?

¿Cuánto?

How much is that? – ¿Cuánto cuesta eso?

How many times do I have to say this? – ¿Cuántas veces debo decir esto?

How much did you miss me? – ¿Cuánto me has extrañado?

How much did you walk today? – ¿Cuánto has caminado hoy?

How much can we spend? – ¿Cuánto podemos gastar?

How much did they steal from you? – ¿Cuánto te han robado?

¿Cuál?

What's the hostel's address? – ¿Cuál es la dirección del hostal?

Which one is your phone? – ¿Cuál es tu teléfono?

Which one is your favorite? – ¿Cuál es tu preferida?

Which car are you talking about? – ¿De cuál automóvil hablas?

What was your best trip? – ¿Cuál fue tu mejor viaje?

What was your worse flight? – ¿Cuál fue tu peor vuelo?

James made an impulsive decision and bought a plane ticket to Mexico, to visit Daniela, the girl he dated shortly in Cartagena. She does not know he is coming to visit, so it is a big shock when he knocks on her door:

DANIELA: My God! What are you doing here? – ¡Dios mío! ¿Qué haces aquí?

JAMES: Happy to see me? – ¿Feliz de verme?

DANIELA: Of course, but I cannot believe it. When did you arrive? – Claro, pero no lo puedo creer. ¿Cuándo llegaste?

JAMES: Like... an hour ago, why? – Como... hace una hora, ¿por qué?

DANIELA: I don't know. Did you come here just to see me? – No lo sé. ¿Has venido aquí para verme?

JAMES: Yes. Is it too crazy? – Sí, ¿es muy loco?

DANIELA: Definitely! Do you know what is even crazier? – ¡Definitivamente! ¿Sabes qué es aún más loco?

JAMES: What? – ¿Qué?

DANIELA: I bought a plane ticket to go see you – Yo compré un billete de avión para ir a verte a ti

JAMES: What? How? Where? – ¿Qué? ¿Cómo? ¿Dónde?

DANIELA: I thought you were going to be in Buenos Aires… I was going to go there in an hour – Pensé que estarías en Buenos Aires… Iba a ir allí en una hora

Conclusion

¡Hola nuevamente!

Did you enjoy this Spanish book and James' love story?

Now you have the basics to understand this beautiful language: its verbal tenses, pronouns, prepositions, and much more.

Dare to challenge yourself and explore Spanish even further until you don't need any book. Read short stories in Spanish, novels, newspapers, websites, watch films, and immerse yourself in as many Spanish-speaking countries as you can.

Try every possible food and learn its ingredients and recipe. Ask locals about their slang, local dishes, and customs. Not only will you end up being fluent in Spanish, but you will also make tons of new friends and get to know much about the world and different cultures. This will definitely make you feel like a richer person.

So, if this is nothing but a starting point, let's hope it was useful for you to take your first steps into this amazing, complex, ever-changing language.

Here are some final tips for you to go all the way with Spanish:

1. Speak from the first day

Unfortunately, many people follow the wrong approach when learning a language. A language is a means of communication and should, therefore, be lived rather than learned. There is no such thing as an "I am ready now." Thus, just jump into the cold water and speak the language at home from day one. It is best to set the goal not to miss a day when you have not used the foreign language in any form. Just try to implement everything you learn directly. So speak, write, and think in your foreign language.

2. Immerse yourself in the foreign language at home

This tip goes hand in hand with the first one. To learn the foreign language quickly and efficiently, you have to integrate it firmly into your everyday life. It is not enough if you learn a few words from time to time and engage in grammar and pronunciation. This has to be done much more intensively. You have to dive properly into the foreign language. Just bring foreign countries to your home. By so-called "immersion", you surround yourself constantly and everywhere with the language.

3. Change the language setting on devices

For example, you could change the menu language of your smartphone or laptop from your native language to the language you are learning. Since you use your smartphone or your laptop every day, you know where to find something and learn some vocabulary along the way. Of course, you can also do the same with your social networks like Facebook and Twitter. However, watch out that you are always able to change back the menu language!

4. Use foreign language media

You could, for example, get a foreign language newspaper. If that is not available or too expensive, then there are enough newspapers or news portals where you can read news online. You are probably already familiar with the news through your native language, and then the context is easier if you reread the same messages in the foreign language. Further aids are foreign-language films or series. It's probably best to start with a movie or series that you've already seen in your native language. Slang and common phrases can make it really hard for you. If you realize that you do not understand it well, try the subtitles in the foreign language. If that does not work, then take the subtitles of your native language and try again. Even music should not be neglected in your foreign-language world. This has the advantage of teaching you much about the pronunciation and emphasis. Incidentally, you are getting a lot closer to the culture of the country.

5. Leave notes in your home

If it does not bother you and others, place sticky notes with words throughout your home. Whether this is your toothbrush, the couch or the remote control, just place notes on as many objects and pieces of furniture as possible with the respective name of the object in the foreign language. As a result, you have the vocabulary all day long and memorize it automatically.

6. Learn the most important phrases

Another helpful tip is to think about what words and phrases you'll need before you travel. For example, you could write down how to reserve a hotel room, book a bus ride, order in a restaurant, ask someone for directions, and communicate with a doctor or the police.

7. Set clear goals

Without goals, you will never get where you want to go. Since you have already booked your flight, you also have a deadline, to which you have reached a goal you have set. To accomplish this, you can now place mini orders. But stay realistic with your goals, especially concerning your mini goals. If they are too big and not realistically achievable, you may lose your courage and give up. A good tip is also that you record your goals in writing because writing is like having a contract with yourself. It makes your goals more binding and makes you feel more obligated to stick to your schedule. Writing things down also has the advantage that you have to formulate your goals more precisely and not forget them so quickly. Do not just try to formulate these goals but really approach and implement them.

8. Humor

Do not feel dejected if it does not work right away. You may be embarrassing yourself in front of a native speaker because you mispronounce a word and form a completely different sense. Nobody will blame you. For most people, it means a lot that you try to learn their language. And when they laugh, they do not mean it negatively. However, the most important thing is: have fun getting to know a new language! After all, you do not have any pressure—as you do at school.

Mastering the foreign language of your destination country only has advantages. You will learn to understand how people of a particular region think, what fears and worries they have, and how they tackle life. You will become more tolerant and see the world differently, and, after your journey, you'll definitely question many ways of thinking regarding your own culture. Of course, you will also learn many new things abroad, even in foreign languages. Make sure to take the time to get familiar with the new language before you leave. It is worth it!

¡Buena suerte!

Annex 1

Who Did What?: Verb Conjugation

This annex is a cheat sheet in case you have to check conjugations quickly!

Present tense

Basic regular verbs ending in -ar

Regular verbs that end in *-ar* always follow the same structure and add the same letters after the root of the verb, as in the following example. For the verb *amar* (*to love*), the root is *am-*.

<u>To love (*amar*)</u>

yo am**o**

tú am**as** / vos am**ás** / usted am**a**

él/ella am**a**

nosotros am**amos**

ustedes am**an** / vosotros am**áis**

ellos/ellas am**an**

Basic regular verbs ending in -er

Regular verbs that end in -er also follow the same structure and add the same letters after the root of the verb, as in the following example. For the verb *temer* (*to fear*), the root is *tem-*.

To fear (*temer*)

yo tem**o**

tú tem**es** / vos tem**és** / usted tem**e**

él/ella tem**e**

nosotros tem**emos**

ustedes tem**en** / vosotros tem**éis**

ellos/ellas tem**en**

Basic regular verbs ending in -ir

Regular verbs that end in -ir also follow the same structure and add the same letters after the root of the verb, as in the following example. For the verb *vivir* (*to live*), the root is *viv-*.

To live (*vivir*)

yo viv**o**

tú viv**es** / vos viv**ís** / usted viv**e**

él/ella viv**e**

nosotros viv**imos**

ustedes viv**en** / vosotros viv**ís**

ellos/ellas viv**en**

To be and to be (*ser y estar*)

Present tense conjugation of the verb to be (*ser*)

yo **soy**

tú **eres** / vos **sos** / usted **es**

él/ella **es**

nosotros **somos**

ustedes **son** / vosotros **sois**

ellos/ellas **son**

Present tense conjugation of the verb to be (*estar*)

yo **estoy**

tú **estás** / vos **estás** / usted **está**

él/ella **está**

nosotros **estamos**

ustedes **están** / vosotros **estáis**

ellos/ellas **están**

The difference with verbs *ser* and *estar* is that *ser* normally refers to a permanent state, while *estar* is more of a passing state. Here are some examples in sentences:

I am Sandra – **Soy** Sandra

I am tired – **Estoy** cansado

You are an idiot – **Eres** un idiota

You are in trouble – **Estás** en problemas

He is a doctor – Él **es** médico

He is running a marathon – Él **está** corriendo una maratón

We are husband and wife –- **Somos** marido y mujer

We are in love – **Estamos** enamorados

You are the best – **Sois** los mejores

You are hiding something – **Estáis** ocultando algo

They are losers – **Son** perdedores

They are coming! – ¡**Están** viniendo!

Other irregular verbs

To have (*tener*)

yo **tengo**

tú **tienes** / vos **tenés** / usted **tiene**

él/ella **tiene**

nosotros **tenemos**

ustedes **tienen** / vosotros **tenéis**

ellos/ellas **tienen**

To say (*decir*)

yo **digo**

tú **dices** / vos **decís** / usted **dice**

él/ella **dice**

nosotros **decimos**

ustedes **dicen** / vosotros **decís**

ellos/ellas **dicen**

To go (*ir*)

yo **voy**

tú **vas** / vos **vas** / usted **va**

él/ella **va**

nosotros **vamos**

ustedes **van** / vosotros **vais**

ellos/ellas **van**

To do (*hacer*)

yo **hago**

tú **haces** / vos **hacés** / usted **hace**

él/ella **hace**

nosotros **hacemos**

ustedes **hacen** / vosotros **hacéis**

ellos/ellas **hacen**

Can (*poder*)

yo **puedo**

tú **puedes** / vos **podés** / usted **puede**

él/ella **puede**

nosotros **podemos**

ustedes **pueden** / vosotros **podéis**

ellos/ellas **pueden**

To see (*ver*)

yo **veo**

tú **ves** / vos **ves** / usted **ve**

él/ella **ve**

nosotros **vemos**

ustedes **ven** / vosotros **veis**

ellos/ellas **ven**

To give (*dar*)

yo **doy**

tú **das** / vos **das** / usted **da**

él/ella **da**

nosotros **damos**

ustedes **dan** / vosotros **dais**

ellos/ellas **dan**

To want (*querer*)

yo **quiero**

tú **quieres** / vos **querés** / usted **quiere**

él/ella **quiere**

nosotros **queremos**

ustedes **quieren** / vosotros **queréis**

ellos/ellas **quieren**

Pretérito perfecto simple

This verbal tense is a past tense equivalent to the English simple past: *I loved, I feared, I lived.*

To love (*amar*)

yo am**é**

tú am**aste** / vos am**aste** / usted am**ó**

él/ella am**ó**

nosotros am**amos**

ustedes am**aron** / vosotros am**asteis**

ellos/ellas ama**ron**

To fear (*temer*)

yo tem**í**

tú tem**iste** / vos tem**iste** / usted tem**ió**

él/ella tem**ió**

nosotros tem**imos**

ustedes tem**ieron** / vosotros tem**isteis**

ellos/ellas tem**ieron**

To live (*vivir*)

yo viv**í**

tú viv**iste** / vos viv**iste** / usted viv**ió**

él/ella viv**ió**

nosotros viv**imos**

ustedes viv**ieron** / vosotros viv**isteis**

ellos/ellas viv**ieron**

Pretérito perfecto compuesto

This past tense is widely used and is equivalent to the English present perfect: *I have loved, I have feared, I have lived*. Instead of using the verb *to have*, Spanish uses a special verb that is only used on this occasion: *haber*. While *haber* is conjugated, the verb remains the same.

To love (*amar*)

yo **he** am**ado**

tú **has** am**ado** / vos **has** am**ado** / usted **ha** am**ado**

él/ella **ha** am**ado**

nosotros **hemos** am**ado**

ustedes **han** am**ado** / vosotros **habéis** am**ado**

ellos/ellas **han** am**ado**

To fear (*temer*)

yo **he** tem**ido**

tú **has** tem**ido** / vos **has** tem**ido** / usted **ha** tem**ido**

él/ella **ha** tem**ido**

nosotros **hemos** tem**ido**

ustedes **han** tem**ido** / vosotros **habéis** tem**ido**

ellos/ellas **han** tem**ido**

To live (*vivir*)

yo **he** viv**ido**

tú **has** viv**ido** / vos **has** viv**ido** / usted **ha** viv**ido**

él/ella **ha** viv**ido**

nosotros **hemos** viv**ido**

ustedes **han** viv**ido** / vosotros **habéis** viv**ido**

ellos/ellas **han** viv**ido**

Pretérito imperfecto

To love (*amar*)

yo am**aba**

tú am**abas** / vos am**abas** / usted am**aba**

él/ella am**aba**

nosotros am**ábamos**

ustedes am**aban** / vosotros am**abais**

ellos/ellas am**aban**

To fear (*temer*)

yo tem**ía**

tú tem**ías** / vos tem**ías** / usted tem**ía**

él/ella tem**ía**

nosotros tem**íamos**

ustedes tem**ían** / vosotros tem**íais**

ellos/ellas tem**ían**

To live (*vivir*)

yo viv**ía**

tú viv**ías** / vos viv**ías** / usted viv**ía**

él/ella viv**ía**

nosotros viv**íamos**

ustedes viv**ía** / vosotros viv**íais**

ellos/ellas viv**ían**

Futuro simple

This verbal tense is equivalent to the English simple future: *I will love, I will fear, I will live.*

To love (*amar*)

yo am**aré**

tú am**arás** / vos am**arás** / usted am**ará**

él/ella am**ará**

nosotros am**aremos**

ustedes am**arán** / vosotros am**aréis**

ellos/ellas am**arán**

To fear (*temer*)

yo tem**eré**

tú tem**erás** / vos tem**erás** / usted tem**erá**

él/ella tem**erá**

nosotros tem**eremos**

ustedes tem**erán** / vosotros tem**eréis**

ellos/ellas tem**erán**

To live (*vivir*)

yo viv**iré**

tú viv**irás** / vos viv**irás** / usted viv**irá**

él/ella viv**irá**

nosotros viv**iremos**

ustedes viv**irán** / vosotros viv**iréis**

ellos/ellas viv**irán**

Estar + gerundio (presente)

To love (*amar*)

yo **estoy** am**ando**

tú **estás** am**ando** / vos **estás** am**ando** / usted **está** am**ando**

él/ella **está** am**ando**

nosotros **estamos** am**ando**

ustedes **están** am**ando** / vosotros **estáis** am**ando**

ellos/ellas **están** am**ando**

To fear (*temer*)

yo **estoy** tem**iendo**

tú **estás** tem**iendo** / vos **estás** tem**iendo** / usted **está** tem**iendo**

él/ella **está** tem**iendo**

nosotros **estamos** tem**iendo**

ustedes **están** tem**iendo** / vosotros **estáis** tem**iendo**

ellos/ellas **están** tem**iendo**

To live (*vivir*)

yo **estoy** viv**iendo**

tú **estás** viv**iendo** / vos **estás** viv**iendo** / usted **está** viv**iendo**

él/ella **está** viv**iendo**

nosotros **estamos** viv**iendo**

ustedes **están** viv**iendo** / vosotros **estáis** viv**iendo**

ellos/ellas **están** viv**iendo**

Exercises

Ahora que vivimos en el campo, finalmente (respirar) .... aire puro.

Los vecinos (vender) .... su casa.

Ella ya tiene todo resuelto, pero yo todavía (decidir) .... qué hacer.

Estar + gerundio (pasado)

To love (*amar*)

yo **estaba** am**ando**

tú **estabas** am**ando** / vos **estabas** am**ando** / usted **estaba** am**ando**

él/ella **estaba** am**ando**

nosotros **estaba** am**ando**

ustedes **estaba** am**ando** / vosotros **estabais** am**ando**

ellos/ellas **estaban** am**ando**

To fear (*temer*)

yo **estaba** tem**iendo**

tú **estabas** tem**iendo** / vos **estabas** tem**iendo** / usted **estaba** tem**iendo**

él/ella **estaba** tem**iendo**

nosotros **estábamos** tem**iendo**

ustedes **estaban** tem**iendo** / vosotros **estabais** tem**iendo**

ellos/ellas **estaban** tem**iendo**

To live (*vivir*)

yo **estaba** viv**iendo**

tú **estabas** viv**iendo** / vos **estabas** viv**iendo** / usted **estaba** viv**iendo**

él/ella **estaba** viv**iendo**

nosotros **estábamos** viv**iendo**

ustedes **estaban** viv**iendo** / vosotros **estabais** viv**iendo**

ellos/ellas **estaban** viv**iendo**

Ir + infinitivo (futuro)

This construction with the conjugated present tense verb *ir* (*to go*) + the infinitive form of the verb is a usual alternative to the simple future.

To love (*amar*)

yo **voy a** am**ar**

tú **vas a** am**ar** / vos **vas a** am**ar** / usted **va a** am**ar**

él/ella **va a** am**ar**

nosotros **vamos a** am**ar**

ustedes **van a** am**ar** / vosotros **vais a** am**ar**

ellos/ellas **van a** am**ar**

To fear (*temer*)

yo **voy a** tem**er**

tú **voy a** tem**er** / vos **voy a** tem**er** / usted **va a** tem**er**

él/ella **va a** tem**er**

nosotros **vamos a** tem**er**

ustedes **van a** tem**er** / vosotros **vais a** tem**er**

ellos/ellas **van a** tem**er**

To live (*vivir*)

yo **voy a** viv**ir**

tú **vas a** viv**ir** / vos **vas a** viv**ir** / usted **va a** viv**ir**

él/ella **va a** viv**ir**

nosotros **vamos a** viv**ir**

ustedes **van a** viv**ir** / vosotros **vais a** viv**ir**

ellos/ellas **van a** viv**ir**

Subjunctive mode

The Spanish subjunctive is used to talk about desires, doubts, the unknown, the abstract, and some emotions. Situations where you have to use it:

1. Sentences with two subjects: sentences with one subject in the main clause and one in the noun clause use the subjunctive.

2. Sentences linked with a relative pronoun: sentences that have parts linked by a relative pronoun (que, quien, como).

3. Sentences that have two verbs and the first one expresses wishes, emotions, impersonal expressions, recommendations, doubt, and denial.

<u>Examples</u>

I need you to **do** something for me – Necesito que **hagas** algo por mí

He wants me to **buy** him the new videogame console – Él quiere que le **compre** la nueva consola de videojuegos

They expect us to **solve** everything – Ellos esperan que nosotros **resolvamos** todo

I doubt he **can** make it – Dudo que él **pueda** hacerlo

I want us to **go** on a trip – Quiero que nos **vayamos** de viaje

She refuses to believe he **is** guilty – Se niega a creer que él **sea** el culpable

We hope you **are** the architect we need – Esperamos que **seas** el arquitecto que necesitamos

I hate that you **talk** to me like that – Odio que me **hables** así

I am glad that you **love** each other again – Me alegra que se **amen** nuevamente

It is necessary that someone **fixes** it – Es necesario que alguien lo **arregle**

He recommended that I **exercise** more – Me recomendó que me **ejercite** más

I wish the food **tastes** as good as it looks – Ojalá la comida **sepa** tan bien como se ve

I wish my son **passes** his driving test – Ojalá mi hijo **apruebe** su examen de conducir

Present subjunctive (*presente del subjuntivo*)

To love (*amar*)

que yo am**e**

que tú am**es** / vos am**es** / usted am**e**

que él/ella am**e**

que nosotros am**emos**

que ustedes am**en** / vosotros am**éis**

que ellos/ellas am**en**

To fear (*temer*)

que yo tem**a**

que tú tem**as** / vos tem**as** / usted tem**a**

que él/ella tem**a**

que nosotros tem**amos**

que ustedes tem**an** / vosotros tem**áis**

que ellos/ellas tem**an**

To live (*vivir*)

que yo viv**a**

que tú viv**as** / vos viv**as** / usted viv**a**

que él/ella viv**a**

que nosotros viv**amos**

que ustedes viv**an** / vosotros viv**áis**

que ellos/ellas viv**an**

To be (*ser*)

que yo **sea**

que tú **seas** / vos **seas** / usted **sea**

que él/ella **sea**

que nosotros **seamos**

que ustedes **sean** / vosotros **seáis**

que ellos/ellas **sean**

To be (*estar*)

que yo **esté**

que tú **estés** / vos **estés** / usted **esté**

que él/ella **esté**

que nosotros **estemos**

que ustedes **estén** / vosotros **estéis**

que ellos/ellas **estén**

To have (*tener*)

que yo **tenga**

que tú **tengas** / vos **tengas** / usted **tenga**

que él/ella **tenga**

que nosotros **tengamos**

que ustedes **tengan** / vosotros **tengáis**

que ellos/ellas **tengan**

To say (*decir*)

que yo **diga**

que tú **digas** / vos **digas** / usted **diga**

que él/ella **diga**

que nosotros **digamos**

que ustedes **digan** / vosotros **digáis**

que ellos/ellas **digan**

To go (*ir*)

que yo **vaya**

que tú **vayas** / vos **vayas** / usted **vaya**

que él/ella **vaya**

que nosotros **vayamos**

que ustedes **vayan** / vosotros **vayáis**

que ellos/ellas **vayan**

To do (*hacer*)

que yo **haga**

que tú **hagas** / vos **hagas** / usted **haga**

que él/ella **haga**

que nosotros **hagamos**

que ustedes **hagan** / vosotros **hagáis**

que ellos/ellas **hagan**

Can (*poder*)

que yo **pueda**

que tú **puedas** / vos **puedas** / usted **pueda**

que él/ella **pueda**

que nosotros **podamos**

que ustedes **puedan** / vosotros **podáis**

que ellos/ellas **puedan**

To see (*ver*)

que yo **vea**

que tú **veas** / vos **veas** / usted **vea**

que él/ella **vea**

que nosotros **veamos**

que ustedes **vean** / vosotros **veáis**

que ellos/ellas **vean**

To give (*dar*)

que yo **dé**

que tú **des** / vos **des** / usted **dé**

que él/ella **dé**

que nosotros **demos**

que ustedes **den** / vosotros **deis**

que ellos/ellas **den**

To want (*querer*)

que yo **quiera**

que tú **quieras** / vos **quieras** / usted **quiera**

que él/ella **quiera**

que nosotros **queramos**

que ustedes **quieran** / vosotros **queráis**

que ellos/ellas **quieran**

Past subjunctive (pretérito imperfecto del subjuntivo)

As previously seen, there are always two forms for this subjunctive tense. You can use either.

To love (*amar*)

que yo am**ara**/am**ase**

que tú am**aras**/am**ases** / vos am**aras**/am**ases** / usted am**ara**/am**ase**

que él/ella am**ara**/am**ase**

que nosotros am**áramos**/am**ásemos**

que ustedes am**aran**/am**asen** / vosotros am**arais**/am**aseis**

que ellos/ellas am**aran**/am**asen**

To fear (*temer*)

que yo tem**iera**/tem**iese**

que tú tem**ieras**/tem**ieses** / vos tem**ieras**/tem**ieses** / usted tem**iera**/tem**iese**

que él/ella tem**iera**/tem**iese**

que nosotros tem**iéramos**/tem**iésemos**

que ustedes tem**ieran**/tem**iesen** / vosotros tem**ierais**/tem**ieseis**

que ellos/ellas tem**ieran**/tem**iesen**

To live (*vivir*)

que yo viv**iera**/viv**iese**

que tú viv**ieras**/viv**ieses** / vos viv**ieras**/viv**ieses** / usted viv**iera**/viv**iese**

que él/ella viv**iera**/viv**iese**

que nosotros viv**iéramos**/viv**iésemos**

que ustedes viv**ieran**/viv**iesen** / vosotros viv**ierais**/viv**ieseis**

que ellos/ellas viv**ieran**/viv**iesen**

To be (*ser*)

que yo **fuera/fuese**

que tú **fueras/fueses** / vos **fueras/fueses** / usted **fuera/fuese** que él/ella **fuera/fuese**

que nosotros **fuéramos/fuésemos**

que ustedes **fueran/fuesen** / vosotros **fuerais/fueseis**

que ellos/ellas **fueran/fuesen**

To be (*estar*)

que yo **estuviera/estuviese**

que tú **estuvieras/estuvieses** / vos **estuvieras/estuvieses** / usted **estuviera/estuviese**

que él/ella **estuviera/estuviese**

que nosotros **estuviéramos/estuviésemos**

que ustedes **estuvieran/estuviesen** / vosotros **estuvierais/estuvieseis**

que ellos/ellas **estuvieran/estuviesen**

To have (*tener*)

que yo **tuviera/tuviese**

que tú **tuvieras/tuvieses** / vos **tuvieras/tuvieses** / usted **tuviera/tuviese**

que él/ella **tuviera/tuviese**

que nosotros **tuviéramos/tuviésemos**

que ustedes **tuvieran/tuviesen** / vosotros **tuvierais/tuvieseis**

que ellos/ellas **tuvieran/tuviesen**

To say (*decir*)

que yo **dijera/dijese**

que tú **dijeras/dijeses** / vos **dijeras/dijeses** / usted **dijera/dijese**

que él/ella **dijera/dijese**

que nosotros **dijéramos/dijésemos**

que ustedes **dijeran/dijesen** / vosotros **dijerais/dijeseis** que ellos/ellas **dijeran/dijesen**

To go (*ir*)

que yo **fuera/fuese**

que tú **fueras/fueses** / vos **fueras/fueses** / usted **fuera/fuese**

que él/ella **fuera/fuese**

que nosotros **fuéramos/fuésemos**

que ustedes **fueran/fuesen** / vosotros **fuerais/fueseis**

que ellos/ellas **fueran/fuesen**

To do (*hacer*)

que yo **hiciera/hiciese**

que tú **hicieras/hicieses** / vos **hicieras/hicieses** / usted **hiciera/hiciese**

que él/ella **hiciera/hiciese**

que nosotros **hiciéramos/hiciésemos**

que ustedes **hicieran/hiciesen** / vosotros **hicierais/hicieseis**

que ellos/ellas **hicieran/hiciesen**

Can (*poder*)

que yo **pudiera/pudiese**

que tú **pudieras/pudieses** / vos **pudieras/pudieses** / usted **pudiera/pudiese**

que él/ella **pudiera/pudiese**

que nosotros **pudiéramos/pudiésemos**

que ustedes **pudieran/pudiesen** / vosotros **pudierais/pudieseis**

que ellos/ellas **pudieran/pudiesen**

To see (*ver*)

que yo **viera/viese**

que tú **vieras/vieses** / vos **vieras/vieses** / usted **viera/viese**

que él/ella **viera/viese**

que nosotros **viéramos/viésemos**

que ustedes **vieran/viesen** / vosotros **vierais/vieseis**

que ellos/ellas **vieran/viesen**

To give (*dar*)

que yo **diera/diese**

que tú **dieras/dieses** / vos **dieras/dieses** / usted **diera/diese**

que él/ella **diera/diese**

que nosotros **diéramos/diésemos**

que ustedes **dieran/diesen** / vosotros **dierais/dieseis**

que ellos/ellas **dieran/diesen**

To want (*querer*)

que yo **quisiera/quisiese**

que tú **quisieras/quisieses** / vos **quisieras/quisieses** / usted **quisiera/quisiese**

que él/ella **quisiera/quisiese**

que nosotros **quisiéramos/quisiésemos**

que ustedes **quisieran/quisiesen** / vosotros **quisierais/quisieseis**

que ellos/ellas **quisieran/quisiesen**

Imperative mood

The Spanish imperative mood is used to give orders. There are no tenses in the imperative mood, but there is an affirmative and a negative form. It is not used with all pronouns since you cannot give orders to yourself or to people who are not there.

As you can see, for the *usted, nosotros,* and *ustedes* forms, the imperative is formed using the forms of the present subjunctive.

Regular verbs

<u>To love (*amar*)</u>

tú am**a** / vos am**á** / usted am**e**

nosotros am**emos**

ustedes am**en** / vosotros am**ad**

<u>To fear (*temer*)</u>

tú tem**e** / vos tem**é** / usted tem**a**

nosotros tem**amos**

ustedes tem**an** / vosotros tem**ed**

<u>To live (*vivir*)</u>

tú viv**e** / vos viv**í** / usted viv**a**

nosotros viv**amos**

ustedes viv**an** / vosotros viv**id**

Irregular verbs

<u>To be (*ser*)</u>

tú **sé** / vos **sé** / usted **sea**

nosotros **seamos**

ustedes **sean** / vosotros **sed**

<u>To be (*estar*)</u>

tú **está** / vos **está** / usted **esté**

que nosotros **estemos**

ustedes **estén** / vosotros **estad**

<u>To have (*tener*)</u>

tú **ten** / vos **tené** / usted **tenga**

nosotros **tengamos**

ustedes **tengan** / vosotros **tened**

<u>To say (*decir*)</u>

tú **di** / vos **decí** / usted **diga**

nosotros **digamos**

ustedes **digan** / vosotros **decid**

<u>To go (*ir*)</u>

tú **ve** / vos **andá** / usted **vaya**

nosotros **vayamos**

ustedes **vayan** / vosotros **id**

<u>To do (*hacer*)</u>

tú **haz** / vos **hacé** / usted **haga**

nosotros **hagamos**

ustedes **hagan** / vosotros **haced**

<u>To give (*dar*)</u>

tú **da** / vos **da** / usted **dé**

nosotros **demos**

ustedes **den** / vosotros **dad**

Imperative + pronouns

It is very common that object pronouns are attached to the imperative verb.

Tell me what you want to do – **Dime** qué quieres hacer

Tell us more about your family – **Cuéntanos** más sobre tu familia

Buy him something to eat – **Cómprale** algo para comer

Sometimes you can even attach two pronouns, an indirect object and a direct object pronoun (always in that order).

Tell it to us – Dínoslo

Bring it to me – Tráemelo

Buy it for you – Cómpratelo

Negative commands

Orders not to do something are formed with the adverb "no" + present subjunctive.

Do not look at me – No me mires

Let's not buy more bread – No compremos más pan

Do not tell me what to do – No me digas qué hacer

Conditional

Just as in English (with *would* and *could*), this tense is used for hypothetical situations and to make polite requests.

I would love to be a millionaire – Me **encantaría** ser millonario

Could I have a glass of water? – ¿**Podría** tomar un vaso de agua?

Could I have your class notes? – ¿Me **prestarías** tus apuntes de la clase?

I would kill for a good slice of pizza – **Mataría** por una buena porción de pizza

To love (*amar*)

yo am**aría**

tú am**arías** / vos am**arías** / usted am**aría**

él/ella am**aría**

nosotros am**arímos**

ustedes am**arían** / vosotros am**aríais**

ellos/ellas am**arían**

To fear (*temer*)

yo tem**ería**

tú tem**erías** / vos tem**erías** / usted tem**ería**

él/ella tem**ería**

nosotros tem**eríamos**

ustedes tem**erían** / vosotros tem**eríais**

ellos/ellas tem**erían**

To live (*vivir*)

yo viv**iría**

tú viv**irías** / vos viv**irías** / usted viv**iría**

él/ella viv**iría**

nosotros viv**iríamos**

ustedes viv**iría** / vosotros viv**iríais**

ellos/ellas viv**irían**

To be (*ser*)

yo **sería**

tú **serías** / vos **serías** / usted **sería**

él/ella **sería**

nosotros **seríamos**

ustedes **serían** / vosotros **seríais**

ellos/ellas **serían**

To be (*estar*)

yo **estaría**

tú **estarías** / vos **estarías** / usted **estaría**

él/ella **estaría**

nosotros **estaríamos**

ustedes **estarían** / vosotros **estaríais**

ellos/ellas **estarían**

To have (*tener*)

yo **tendría**

tú **tendrías** / vos **tendrías** / usted **tendría**

él/ella **tendría**

nosotros **tendríamos**

ustedes **tendrían** / vosotros **tendríais**

ellos/ellas **tendrían**

To say (*decir*)

yo **diría**

tú **dirías** / vos **dirías** / usted **diría**

él/ella **diría**

nosotros **diríamos**

ustedes **dirían** / vosotros **diríais**

ellos/ellas **dirían**

To go (*ir*)

yo **iría**

tú **irías** / vos **irías** / usted **iría**

él/ella **iría**

nosotros **iríamos**

ustedes **irían** / vosotros **iríais**

ellos/ellas **irían**

To do (*hacer*)

yo **haría**

tú **harías** / vos **harías** / usted **haría**

él/ella **haría**

nosotros **haríamos**

ustedes **harían** / vosotros **haríais**

ellos/ellas **harían**

Can (*poder*)

yo **podría**

tú **podrías** / vos **podrías** / usted **podría**

él/ella **podría**

nosotros **podríamos**

ustedes **podrían** / vosotros **podríais**

ellos/ellas **podrían**

To see (*ver*)

yo **vería**

tú **verías** / vos **verías** / usted **vería**

él/ella **vería**

nosotros **veríamos**

ustedes **verían** / vosotros **veríais**

ellos/ellas **verían**

To give (*dar*)

yo **daría**

tú **darías** / vos **darías** / usted **daría**

él/ella **daría**

nosotros **daríamos**

ustedes **darían** / vosotros **daríais**

ellos/ellas **darían**

To want (*querer*)

yo **querría**

tú **querrías** / vos **querrías** / usted **querría**

él/ella **querría**

nosotros **querríamos**

ustedes **querrían** / vosotros **querríais**

ellos/ellas **querrían**

Past subjunctive + conditional

Conditional sentences use the past subjunctive and the conditional tense. Just as in English when you use *if* to introduce this kind of sentence, in Spanish, *si* is used, which is different from *sí* (*yes*) because it does not have a *tilde*.

If I **were** rich, I **would buy** you a mansion – Si yo **fuera** rico, te **compraría** una mansión

If they **had** any brains, they **would stay away** from that scam – Si **tuvieran** cerebro, **se alejarían** de esa estafa

If I **had** the time, I **could start** a new major – Si **tuviera** tiempo, **podría** comenzar una nueva carrera

Annex 2

Tildes: Writing in Spanish Like a Pro

As you have probably noticed before, in Spanish, a little mark is placed on top of vowels to accentuate them: *á, é, í, ó, ú*. In Spanish, this means you have to stress (accentuate) the word where the mark (the *tilde*) is.

It is not the same to say *estas* (*these*) than to say *estás* (*you are*). In the first case, you stress the first syllable and, in the second case, you stress the final syllable.

The basic rules for accentuating might sound a bit complicated now, but they are actually simpler than they seem. You do not need to learn these by heart to understand or speak Spanish, but they are useful if you want to learn how to write properly.

1- If the word is stressed on the last syllable, you have to write the *tilde* when it ends in a vowel, an *s* or an *n*: *estás* (*you are*), *colibrí* (*hummingbird*), *perdió* (*he lost*), *colchón* (*mattress*). If they end in any other letter, they are still stressed in the last syllable, but you do not have to write the *tilde*: *borrar* (*to erase*), *motor* (*engine*), *feliz* (*happy*).

2- If the word is stressed on the second to last syllable, you have to write the *tilde* when it ends in any letter *but* a vowel, an *s* or an *n*: *árbol* (*tree*), *lápiz* (*pencil*), *útil* (*useful*). If they end in a vowel, an *s* or an *n*, these words are still stressed in the second to last syllable, but you do not have to write the *tilde*: *alegre* (*cheerful*), *amarillo* (*yellow*), *beso* (*kiss*).

3- If the word is stressed on any syllable before the second to last, it always has to have a *tilde*: *murciélago* (*bat*), *física* (*physics*), *gramática* (*grammar*), *matemática* (*math*).

There are a few **exceptions**.

Adverbs that end in -*mente* (-*ly*) do not always follow the third rule. They keep the accentuation of the original word, as if the -*mente* suffix were not there, even though they are always stressed in the second to last syllable: *claramente* (*clearly*), *velozmente* (*quickly*), *últimamente* (*lately*).

Another exception is that vowels *i* and *u* always have to carry a *tilde* when they are stressed and come before or after vowels *a*, *e* or *o*: *raíz* (*root*), *país* (*country*), *baúl* (*trunk*), *freír* (*to fry*), *sandía* (*watermelon*), *frío* (*cold*).

Annex 3

Words and Sentences Everyone Needs to Know

Everyday words

sí – yes

no – no

por favor – please

gracias – thank you

permiso – excuse me

¿disculpe? – pardon?

lo siento/perdón – I'm sorry

¿dónde? – where?

¿por qué? – why?

¿cuándo? – when?

¿quién? – who?

¿cómo? – how?

aquí – here

allí – there

Understanding

Comprendo – I understand

No comprendo – I don't understand

Por favor, hable más despacio – Please, speak slowly

¿Podría repetir eso, por favor? – Could you repeat that, please?

¿Podría escribir eso, por favor? – Could you write that down, please?

¿Habla Inglés? – Do you speak English?

¿Habla Español? – Do you speak Spanish?

¿Habla Francés? – Do you speak French?

¿Habla Alemán? – Do you speak German?

¿Habla Italiano? – Do you speak Italian?

Signs

abierto – open

cerrado – closed

entrada – entrance

salida – exit

empuje – push

tire – pull

hombres – men

mujeres – women

ocupado – occupied

libre – vacant

Greetings

¿Cómo estás/está? (informal/formal speech) – How are you?

Bien – Well

Bastante bien – Quite well

No tan bien – Not so good

Hola – Hello

Buen día – Good morning

Buenas tardes – Good afternoon/evening

Buenas noches – Night

Chau – Bye

Adiós – Goodbye

¿Cómo te llamas? – What is your name?

Mi nombre es… – My name is…

¿De dónde eres? – Where are you from?

Yo soy de… – I'm from…

Hasta luego – See you later

Tenga un buen día – Have a nice day

¡Buen fin de semana! – Have a good weekend!

Cuídate – Take care

Igualmente – You too

Nos vemos – See you

To apologize/thank someone

Perdón – Sorry

Lo lamento – I am sorry

Gracias – Thanks

Muchas gracias – Thank you very much

De nada – You are welcome

No hay por qué – Never mind

Está bien – It's fine

Compliments

Eso se ve muy bien – That looks good

Eres muy amable – You are very nice

Te ves muy bien – You look really good

¡Buen trabajo! – Good job!

¡Bien hecho! – Well done!

How are you?

¿Cómo estás tú? / ¿Cómo está usted? (informal/formal) – How are you/you?

Estoy bien – I'm fine

Bien, ¿y tú? – Good, and you?

No me estoy sintiendo bien – I am not feeling well

Asking for internet and Wi-Fi

¿Tiene internet aquí? – Do you have internet access here?

¿Tiene Wi-Fi aquí? – Do you have Wi-Fi here?

¿Cuál es la contraseña para usar internet? – What's the password for the internet?

Asking for opinions and expressing yourself

¿Qué piensas? – What do you think?

Creo que… – I think that…

Espero que… – I hope that…

Temo que… – I'm afraid that…

En mi opinión… – In my opinion…

Estoy de acuerdo – I agree

No estoy de acuerdo – I disagree

Es cierto – That's true

No es cierto – That's not true

Creo que sí – I think so

No lo creo – I don't think so

Espero que sí – I hope so

Espero que no – I hope not

Tienes razón – You're right

Estás equivocado – You're wrong

No me importa – I don't mind

Depende de ti – It's up to you

Eso depende – That depends

Eso es interesante – That's interesting

Eso es gracioso – That's funny

Getting to know each other

¿Cómo te llamas? – What is your name?

Me llamo… – My name is…

¿De dónde eres? – Where are you from?

Soy de… – I'm from…

¿De qué trabajas? – What do you do for work?

Soy… – I am…

¿Desde cuándo estás en…? – Since when are you in…?

¿Conoces…? – Do you know…?

Make an appointment

¿Quieres ir al cine mañana? – Do you want to go to the cinema tomorrow?

Vayamos al cine mañana – Let's go to the cinema tomorrow

¿A qué hora nos encontraremos? – When/At what time are we meeting?

¿Tienes tiempo mañana? – Do you have free time tomorrow?

Llámame… – Call me

Days of the week

Lunes – Monday

Martes – Tuesday

Miércoles – Wednesday

Jueves – Thursday

Viernes – Friday

Sábado – Saturday

Domingo – Sunday

Months

Enero – January

Febrero – February

Marzo – March

Abril – April

Mayo – May

Junio – June

Julio – July

Agosto – August

Septiembre – September

Octubre – October

Noviembre – November

Diciembre – December

Directions

¿Cómo llego a…? – How do I get to…?

…la estación central de trenes? – …the train station?

…la estación central de buses? – …the bus station?

…el aeropuerto? – …the airport?

…el centro? – …downtown?

…el hostal? – …the hostel?

…el hotel…? – …the… hotel?

…el consulado? – …the consulate?

¿Dónde puedo encontrar… – Where are there…

…hoteles? – …hotels?

…restaurantes? – …restaurants?

…bares? – …bars?

…buenas vistas? – …sights to see?

¿Me lo puede mostrar en el mapa? – Can you show me on the map?

calle – street

Gire a la izquierda – Turn left

Gire a la derecha – Turn right

izquierda – left

derecha – right

derecho – straight ahead

hacia el/la… – towards the…

después del/de la… – past the…

antes del/de la… – before the…

norte – north

sur – south

este – east

oeste – west

en subida – uphill

en bajada – downhill

Taxi

¡Taxi! – Taxi!

Lléveme a…, por favor – Take me to…, please.

¿Cuánto cuesta ir hasta…? – How much does it cost to get to…?

Lléveme allí, por favor – Take me there, please.

¿Qué tan largo es el viaje? – How long will the journey take?

¿Le molesta si abro la ventana? – Do you mind if I open the window?

¿Le molesta si cierro la ventana? – Do you mind if I close the window?

¿Ya estamos cerca? – Are we almost there?

¿Cuánto es? – How much is it?

Guarde el cambio – That's fine, keep the change

¿Le gustaría un recibo? – Would you like a receipt?

¿Me puede dar el recibo, por favor? – Could I have a receipt, please?

¿Podría pasarme a buscar a las…? – Could you pick me up here at… (time)?

¿Podría esperarme aquí? – Could you wait for me here?

¿Dónde está? – Where are you?

¿Cuál es la dirección? – What's the address?

Estoy en… – I'm at…

el hotel – the hotel

la estación central – the train station

¿Cuál es su nombre? – Could I take your name, please?

¿Cuánto tengo que esperar? – How long will I have to wait?

¿Cuánto tiempo tomará? – How long will it be?

Está en camino – It's on its way

¿A dónde le gustaría ir? – Where would you like to go?

Me gustaría ir a… – I'd like to go to…

A la estación central – to the train station

¿Podría llevarme a…? – Could you take me to…?

el centro de la ciudad – the city center

¿Cuánto cuesta ir hasta…? – How much would it cost to go to…?

el aeropuerto – the airport

¿Podemos detenernos en un cajero automático? – Could we stop at a cashpoint?

¿El taxímetro está funcionando? – Is the meter switched on?

Por favor, inicie el taxímetro – Please, switch the meter on

Passport control and customs

¿Puedo ver su pasaporte, por favor? – Could I see your passport, please?

¿Desde dónde viaja? – Where have you traveled from?

¿Cuál es el motivo de su visita? – What's the purpose of your visit?

Estoy de vacaciones – I'm on holiday

Estoy en un viaje de negocios – I'm on business

Estoy visitando a familiares – I'm visiting relatives

¿Por cuánto tiempo se quedará? – How long will you be staying?

¿Dónde se quedará? – Where will you be staying?

formulario de inmigración – immigration form

¡Disfrute su estadía! – Enjoy your stay!

¿Puede abrir su maleta, por favor? – Could you open your bag, please?

¿Tiene algo que declarar? – Do you have anything to declare?

Tiene que pagar impuestos por estos bienes – You have to pay duty on these items

Finding accommodation

Estamos buscando alojamiento – We're looking for accommodation

Necesitamos un lugar donde dormir – We need somewhere to stay

¿Tiene una lista de…? – Do you have a list of…?

hoteles – hotels

bed and breakfasts – bed and breakfasts

hostales – hostels

campamentos – campsites

¿Qué tipo de alojamiento está buscando? – What sort of accommodation are you looking for?

¿Puede reservar alojamiento para mí? – Can you book accommodation for me?

Reservation

¿Puedo ver su pasaporte? – Could I see your passport?

¿Puede completar esta planilla? – Could you please fill in this registration form?

¿Tiene habitaciones disponibles? – Do you have any rooms available?

¿Cuánto cuesta un cuarto para una persona/dos personas? – How much is a room for one person/two people?

¿El cuarto cuenta con… – Does the room come with…

…un baño? – …a bathroom?

…un teléfono? – …a telephone?

…una TV? – …a TV?

¿Puedo ver la habitación antes? – May I see the room first?

¿Tiene algo menos ruidoso? – Do you have anything quieter?

…más pequeño? – …smaller?

…más grande? – …bigger?

…más limpio? – …cleaner?

…más barato? – …cheaper?

Okay, ¡lo tomo! – Okay, I'll take it

Me quedaré por… noche/s – I will stay for… night/s

¿Puede sugerirme otro hotel? – Can you suggest another hotel?

¿Tiene caja fuerte? – Do you have a safe?

…armarios? – …lockers?

¿El desayuno está incluido? – Is breakfast/supper included?

¿A qué hora es el desayuno/la cena? – What time is breakfast/supper?

¿Puedo tomar el desayuno en mi habitación, por favor? – Could I have breakfast in my room, please?

¿A qué hora cierra el bar? – What time does the bar close?

¿Podría ayudarlo con su equipaje? – Would you like any help with your luggage?

Por favor, ¿podría limpiar mi habitación? – Could you please clean my room?

¿Podría despertarme a las...? – Can you wake me at...?

Quiero hacer el check out – I want to check out

¿Dónde están los ascensores? – Where are the elevators?

Creo que hay un error en la cuenta – I think there's a mistake in this bill

¿Cómo le gustaría pagar? – How would you like to pay?

Pagaré... – I'll pay...

con tarjeta de crédito – by credit card

en efectivo – in cash

¿Ha usado el minibar? – Have you used the minibar?

No hemos usado el minibar – We haven't used the minibar

¿Puede alguien ayudarnos a bajar nuestro equipaje? – Could we have some help bringing our luggage down?

¿Tiene sitio para que guardemos nuestro equipaje? – Do you have anywhere we could leave our luggage?

¿Puede darme un recibo, por favor? – Could I have a receipt, please?

¿Puede llamar un taxi, por favor? – Could you please call me a taxi?

Espero que haya pasado una agradable estadía/estancia – I hope you had an enjoyable stay

Realmente disfruté mi estadía/estancia – I've really enjoyed my stay

Realmente disfrutamos nuestra estadía/estancia – We've really enjoyed our stay

Camping

campamento – campsite

tienda – tent

autocaravana – caravan

casa rodante – motorhome

¿Tiene parcelas libres? – Do you have any pitches free?

¿Puedo aparcar junto a la parcela? – Can I park beside the pitch?

parcela con servicios – serviced pitch

parcela sin servicios – unserviced pitch

conexión eléctrica – electrical connection

¿Cuál es el costo por noche? – What is the charge per night?

¿Dónde están las duchas? – Where are the showers?

¿Dónde está la lavandería? – Where are the laundry facilities?

¿Esta es agua potable? – Is this drinking water?

¿Puedo pedirle una garrafa? – Can I borrow a gas cylinder?

Complaints

Me gustaría otra habitación – I would like a different room

No funciona la calefacción – The heating does not work

El aire acondicionado no funciona – The air conditioning does not work

La habitación es muy ruidosa – The room is very noisy

La habitación huele mal – The room smells bad

Pedí una habitación para no fumadores – I requested a non-smoking room

Pedí una habitación con vista – I requested a room with a view

Mi llave no funciona – My key does not work

La ventana no abre – The window does not open

La habitación no ha sido limpiada – The room has not been cleaned

Hay ratones/ratas/insectos en la habitación – There are mice/rats/bugs in the room

No hay agua caliente – There is no hot water

No recibí mi llamada de despertador – I did not receive my wake-up call

Hay gastos de más en mi cuenta – The bill is overcharged

Mi vecino hace demasiado ruido – My neighbor is too loud

entrada – check-in

salida – check-out

reserva – reservation

habitación disponible – vacant room

reservar – to book

registrarse – to check in

salir/hacer checkout – to check out

pagar la cuenta – to pay the bill

quedarse en un hotel – to stay at a hotel

hotel – hotel

bed and breakfast – B&B

casa de huéspedes – guesthouse

hostel – hostel

campamento – campsite

habitación simple – single room

habitación doble – double room

habitación doble con camas separadas – twin room

habitación con tres camas – triple room

suite – suite

aire acondicionado – air conditioning

baño – toilet

baño en suite – en-suite bathroom (separate bathroom)

acceso a internet – internet access

minibar – minibar

caja fuerte – safe

ducha – shower

bar – bar

estacionamiento/aparcadero – parking lot

pasillo/corredor – corridor

salida de incendio – fire escape

habitación de juegos – games room

gimnasio – gym

servicio de lavandería – laundry service

ascensor – lift

vestíbulo – lobby

recepción – reception

restaurante – restaurant

servicio a la habitación – room service

sauna – sauna

piscina – swimming pool

encargado/a – manager

empleado/a de limpieza – housekeeper

recepcionista – receptionist

portero – doorman

alarma de incendios – fire alarm

lavandería – laundry

llave de la habitación – room key

número de la habitación – room number

llamada de despertador – wake-up call

Money

¿Acepta dólares americanos? – Do you accept American dollars?

¿Acepta libras esterlinas? – Do you accept British pounds?

¿Acepta euros? – Do you accept Euros?

¿Acepta tarjeta de crédito? – Do you accept credit cards?

¿Puede cambiar dinero para mí? – Can you change money for me?

¿Dónde puedo cambiar dinero? – Where can I get money changed?

¿Puede cambiar un cheque de viajero para mí? – Can you change a traveler's check for me?

¿Dónde puedo cambiar un cheque de viajero? – Where can I get a traveler's check changed?

¿Cuál es la tasa de cambio? – What is the exchange rate?

¿Dónde hay un cajero automático? – Where is an ATM?

Me gustaría cambiar dinero – I'd like to change some money

¿Cuál es la tasa de cambio para euros/dólares? – What's the exchange rate for euros/dollars?

Me gustaría cambiar… – I'd like to change some…

euros – euros

dólares estadounidenses – US dollars

¿Dónde está el cajero automático más cercano? – Where's the nearest cash machine?

Perdí mi tarjeta de banco – I've lost my bank card

Quiero informar… – I want to report a…

una tarjeta de crédito perdida – lost credit card

una tarjeta de crédito robada – stolen credit card

He olvidado mi contraseña de banco en línea – I've forgotten my internet banking password

He olvidado mi número de PIN – I've forgotten my PIN number

Inserte su tarjeta – Insert your card

Ingrese su número de PIN – Enter your PIN

PIN incorrecto – Incorrect PIN

Ingresar – Enter

Correcto – Correct

Cancelar – Cancel

Retirar dinero – Withdraw cash

Otro monto – Other amount

Por favor, espere – Please, wait

Fondos insuficientes – Insufficient funds

Saldo – Balance

Impreso – Printed

¿Desea un recibo? – Would you like a receipt?

Remover tarjeta – Remove card

Salir – Quit

Reservation and ordering

Una mesa para uno/dos, por favor – A table for one person/two people, please

¿Puedo ver el menú, por favor? – Can I look at the menu, please?

¿Puedo ver la cocina? – Can I look in the kitchen?

¿Hay una especialidad de la casa? – Is there a house specialty?

¿Hay una especialidad local? – Is there a local specialty?

Soy vegetariano/a – I'm a vegetarian

No como cerdo – I don't eat pork

No como carne de vaca – I don't eat beef

Solo como comida kosher – I only eat kosher food

a la carta – a la carte

desayuno – breakfast

almuerzo – lunch

merienda – teatime

cena – dinner

Me gustaría… – I would like…

Quiero un platillo que tenga… – I want a dish containing…

pollo – chicken

res – beef

pescado – fish

jamón – ham

salchichas – sausages

queso – cheese

huevos – eggs

ensalada – salad

vegetales – vegetables

fruta – fruit

pan – bread

tostadas – toast

fideos – noodles

pasta – pasta

arroz – rice

frijoles – beans

papas – potatoes

¿Puedo tomar un vaso de…? – May I have a glass of…?

¿Puedo tomar una copa de…? – May I have a cup of…?

¿Puedo tomar una botella de…? – May I have a bottle of…?

café – coffee

té – tea

jugo/zumo – juice

agua – water

cerveza – beer

vino tinto/blanco – red/white wine

¿Podría darme…? – May I have some…?

sal – salt

pimienta – black pepper

manteca – butter

¿Disculpe, mesero/camarero/mozo? – Excuse me, waiter?

He terminado – I'm finished

Estaba delicioso – It was delicious

Por favor, levante los platos – Please, clear the plates

La cuenta, por favor – The check, please

Ordering snacks

¿Tiene bocadillos? – Do you have any snacks?

¿Tiene sándwiches? – Do you have any sandwiches?

¿Sirven comida? – Do you serve food?

¿A qué hora cierra la cocina? – What time does the kitchen close?

¿Aún se sirve comida aquí? – Are you still serving food?

Unas patatas fritas de paquete, por favor – A packet of crisps, please

¿Qué sabor le gustaría? – What flavor would you like?

saladas – salted

queso y cebolla – cheese and onion

sal y vinagre – salt and vinegar

¿Qué tipo de sándwiches tienen? – What sort of sandwiches do you have?

¿Tienen platos calientes? – Do you have any hot food?

Los especiales del día están en la pizarra – Today's specials are on the board

¿Es servicio a la carta o autoservicio? – Is it table service or self-service?

¿Qué le puedo traer? – What can I get you?

¿Quiere algo de comer? – Would you like anything to eat?

¿Puedo ver un menú, por favor? – Could we see a menu, please?

¿Para llevar o para comer aquí? – Eat in or take away?

fresco – fresh

viejo – moldy

podrido – rotten

jugoso – juicy

maduro – ripe

verde – unripe

tierno – tender

duro – tough

quemado – burnt

pasado – overcooked

crudo – underdone/raw

bien cocido – well done

delicioso – delicious

horrible – horrible

salado – salty

salado – savory

dulce – sweet

agrio – sour

sabroso – tasty

picante – spicy/hot

suave – mild

hornear – to bake

hervir – to boil

freir – to fry

grillar – to grill

rostizar – to roast

cocinar al vapor – to steam

desayuno – breakfast

almuerzo – lunch

merienda – teatime

cena – dinner

desayunar – to have breakfast

almorzar – to have lunch

cenar – to have dinner

ingrediente – ingredient

receta – recipe

cocinar – to cook

poner la mesa – to set the table

levantar/recoger la mesa – to clear the table

sentarse a la mesa – to come to the table

limpiar la mesa – to wipe the table

preparar una comida – to prepare a meal

el bar – the bar

cocinero/chef – cook/chef

reserva – reservation

menú – menu

mesero/camarero/mozo – waiter

mesera/camarera/moza – waitress

carta de vinos – wine list

entrante/entrada/aperitivo – starter

plato principal – main course

postre – dessert

servicio – service

cobro de servicio – service charge

propina – tip

bars – bars

You can easily order your favorite drinks in a bar if you use the phrases below!

Ordering drinks

¿Se sirve alcohol? – Do you serve alcohol?

¿Hay servicio de mesa? – Is there table service?

Una cerveza/dos cervezas, por favor – A beer/two beers, please

Un vaso de vino tinto/blanco, por favor – A glass of red/white wine, please

Un vaso, por favor – A glass, please

Una pinta, por favor – A pint, please

Una botella, por favor – A bottle, please

whisky – whiskey

vodka – vodka

ron – rum

agua – water

soda – soda

agua tónica – tonic water

jugo/zumo de naranja – orange juice

¿Tiene bocadillos? – Do you have any bar snacks?

Uno más, por favor – One more, please

Otra ronda, por favor – Another round, please

¿Cuándo cierra el bar? – When is closing time?

¿Qué le gustaría beber? – What would you like to drink?

¿Qué va a pedir? – What are you having?

¿Qué le puedo traer? – What can I get you?

Voy a querer…, por favor – I'll have…, please

una pinta de cerveza – a pint of lager

una copa de vino blanco – a glass of white wine

una copa de vino tinto – a glass of red wine

un jugo de naranja – an orange juice

un café – a coffee

una cola/una Coca Cola – a Coke

una Coca Cola Light – a Diet Coke

¿Grande o pequeño/a? – Large or small?

¿Lo quiere con hielo? – Would you like ice with that?

Sin hielo, por favor – No ice, please

Un poco, por favor – A little, please

Mucho hielo, por favor – Lots of ice, please

Una cerveza, por favor – A beer, please

Dos cervezas, por favor – Two beers, please

Tres chupitos de tequila, por favor – Three shots of tequila, please

¿Ya está atendido? – Are you already being served?

Estamos atendidos, gracias – We're being served, thanks

¿Quién sigue? – Who's next?

¿Qué vino le gustaría? – Which wine would you like?

El vino de la casa está bien – House wine is fine

¿Qué cerveza le gustaría? – Which beer would you like?

¿Le gustaría cerveza tirada o en botella? – Would you like draught or bottled beer?

Lo mismo para mí, por favor – I'll have the same, please

Nada para mí, gracias – Nothing for me, thanks

Quiero esto – I'll get this

¡Quédese con el cambio! – Keep the change!

¡Salud! – Cheers!

¿A quién le toca pagar la ronda? – Whose round is it?

Me toca pagar la ronda – It's my round

Te toca pagar la ronda – It's your round

Otra cerveza, por favor – Another beer, please

Dos cervezas más, por favor – Another two beers, please

Lo mismo otra vez, por favor – Same again, please

¿Aún sirven bebidas? – Are you still serving drinks?

¡Última ronda! – Last orders!

Asking for internet and Wi-Fi

¿Tiene internet aquí? – Do you have internet access here?

¿Tiene Wi-Fi aquí? – Do you have Wi-Fi here?

¿Cuál es la contraseña para usar internet? – What's the password for the internet?

Me siento bien – I feel fine

Me siento terrible – I feel terrible

Tengo resaca – I've got a hangover

¡Nunca beberé de nuevo! – I'm never going to drink again!

Smoking

¿Fumas? – Do you smoke?

No, no fumo – No, I don't smoke

Lo he dejado – I've given up

¿Te molesta si fumo? – Do you mind if I smoke?

¿Quieres un cigarrillo? – Would you like a cigarette?

¿Tienes un encendedor? – Have you got a lighter?

Shopping

¿Tiene esto en mi talla? – Do you have this in my size?

¿Cuánto cuesta esto? – How much is this?

Es demasiado caro – That's too expensive

¿Aceptaría…? – Would you take…?

caro – expensive

barato – cheap

No me alcanza – I don't have enough

No lo quiero – I don't want it

Me está estafando – You're cheating me

No me interesa – I'm not interested

Okay, lo llevo – Okay, I'll take it

¿Tiene una bolsa? – Can I have a bag?

¿Hace envíos? – Do you ship?

¿Tiene tallas grandes? – Do you stock large sizes?

Necesito… – I need…

dentífrico – toothpaste

un cepillo de dientes – a toothbrush

tampones – tampons

jabón – soap

shampoo/champú – shampoo

analgésicos – pain reliever

medicina para el resfrío – cold medicine

medicina para el estómago – stomach medicine

una afeitadora – a razor

un paraguas – an umbrella

protector/loción solar – sun lotion

una postal – a postcard

estampillas – stamps

un cargador de teléfono – a phone charger

un adaptador – a power adaptor

baterías – batteries

una pluma – a pen

Le queda bien – It suits you

Le quedan bien – They suit you

¿Lo tiene en otros colores? – Do you have it in different colors?

Me gustan – I like them

No me gustan – I don't like them

No me gusta el color – I don't like the color

¿De qué están hechos? – What are these made of?

¿Pueden lavarse? – Are these washable?

No, deben ser lavados en seco – No, they have to be dry-cleaned

Lo llevo – I'll take it

Los llevo – I'll take them

Llevo este – I'll take this one

Llevo estos – I'll take these

Finding products

¿Podría decirme dónde está el/la…? – Could you tell me where the… is?

la leche – milk

la panadería – bread counter

la sección de carnes – meat section

la sección de congelados – frozen food section

¿Está atendido/a? – Are you being served?

Me gustaría… – I'd like…

ese trozo de queso – that piece of cheese

una porción de pizza – a slice of pizza

seis rodajas de jamón – six slices of ham

aceitunas – some olives

¿Cuánto le gustaría? – How much would you like?

300 gramos – 300 grams

medio kilo – half a kilo

Son $3.247 (tres mil doscientos cuarenta y siete pesos) – that's $3,247

At a hair salon

Me gustaría un corte de cabello, por favor – I'd like a haircut, please

¿Es necesario hacer una reserva? – Do I need to book?

¿Está disponible ahora? – Are you able to see me now?

¿Quiere que le lave el cabello? – Would you like me to wash your hair?

¿Qué le gustaría? – What would you like?

¿Cómo quiere que se lo corte? – How would you like me to cut it?

Como usted quiera – However you want

Me gustaría… – I'd like…

un recorte – a trim

un nuevo estilo – a new style

una permanente – a perm

un flequillo – a fringe

reflejos/mechas – some highlights

una tintura – it colored

¿Qué tan corto lo desea? – How short would you like it?

no demasiado corto – not too short

bastante corto – quite short

muy corto – very short

nivel uno – grade one

nivel dos – grade two

nivel tres – grade three

nivel cuatro – grade four

completamente rasurado – completely shaven

Así está bien, gracias – That's fine, thanks

¿Qué color le gustaría? – What color would you like?

¿Cuál de estos colores desea? – Which of these colors would you like?

¿Podría recortar mi barba, por favor? – Could you trim my beard, please?

¿Cuánto es? – How much is it?

barato – cheap

cliente – customer

descuento – discount

caro – expensive

precio – price

rebajas – sale

tienda – shop

bolsa de compras – shopping bag

lista de compras – shopping list

oferta especial – special offer

comprar – to buy

vender – to sell

pedir – to order

ir de compras – to go shopping

pasillo – aisle

cesta – basket

caja – counter

probador – fitting room

encargado – manager

estante – shelf

asistente de compras – shop assistant

vidriera – shop window

carrito – trolley

cajero – cashier

efectivo – cash

cambio – change

caja – checkout

queja – complaint

tarjeta de crédito – credit card

agotado – out of stock

bolsa de plástico – plastic bag

bolso/cartera – purse

fila/cola – queue

recibo – receipt

devolución/reintegro – refund

caja – till

cartera/billetera – wallet

Driving

¿Puedo alquilar un automóvil? – Can I rent a car?

¿Tiene seguro? – Do you have insurance?

pare – stop

un sentido – one way

ceda el paso – yield

no estacionar/prohibido estacionar – no parking

límite de velocidad – speed limit

estación de servicio/gasolinera – gas station

gasolina/combustible/nafta – petrol/gas

diésel – diesel

auto/coche/automóvil – car

caja de cambios – gear stick

transmisión automática – automatic transmission

calle principal – main road

autopista – highway

calle de un solo sentido – one-way street

calle – road

esquina – corner

cruce – crossroads/junction

bifurcación – fork

paso a nivel – level crossing

acera – pavement/sidewalk

paso peatonal – pedestrian crossing

señal de tránsito – road sign

banquina – roadside

rotonda – roundabout

servicios – services

letrero – signpost

límite de velocidad – speed limit

semáforo – traffic light

giro – turn

accidente – accident

neumático pinchado – flat tire

niebla – fog

multa por exceso de velocidad – speeding fine

embotellamiento – traffic jam

chocar – to crash

choque – crash

tener un accidente – to have an accident

instructor de manejo – driving instructor

lección de manejo – driving lesson

licencia de conducir – driving license

escuela de manejo – driving school

examen de manejo – driving test

estacionamiento/aparcadero – car park

aparcar/estacionar – to park

parquímetro – parking meter

multa – ticket

lavadero – car wash

diésel – diesel

aceite – oil

bicicleta – bike

bus – bus

autocaravana – caravan

motocicleta/moto – motorbike

taxi – taxi

camión – truck

auto de alquiler – rented car

llaves del auto – car keys

ciclista – cyclist

conductor – driver

garaje – garage

mecánico – mechanic

seguro – insurance

pasajero – passenger

peatón – pedestrian

reversa – reverse gear

mapa – road map

GPS (ge pe ese) – GPS

velocidad – speed

tráfico – traffic

vehículo – vehicle

acelerar – to accelerate

frenar – to brake

conducir – to drive

bajar la velocidad – to slow down

aumentar la velocidad – to speed up

acelerador – accelerator

pedal de freno – brake pedal

freno de mano – handbrake

volante – steering wheel

batería – battery

motor – engine

caño de escape – exhaust pipe

limpiaparabrisas – windscreen wiper

aire acondicionado – air conditioning

cierre centralizado – central locking

luces de freno – brake lights

espejo retrovisor – rearview mirror

asiento trasero – back seat

asiento para niños – child seat

asiento delantero – front seat

tanque de combustible – fuel tank

patente/placa – plate

número de patente/placa – plate number

cinturón de seguridad – seat belt

rueda de auxilio – spare wheel

ventana – window

parabrisas – windscreen

Emergencies

¡Ayuda! – Help!

¡Fuego! – Fire!

¡Vete! – Go away!

Llamaré a la policía – I'll call the police

¡Es urgente! – It's urgent!

Estoy perdido – I'm lost

He perdido… – I've lost…

mi pasaporte – my passport

las llaves de mi automóvil – my car keys

Me han robado – I've been robbed

He tenido un accidente – I've had an accident

Se ha roto mi auto – My car has broken down

Mi coche ha sido robado – My car has been stolen

Necesito… – I need…

combustible – petrol

un mecánico – a mechanic

a la policía – the police

Health

Necesito… – I need…

un doctor – a doctor

un teléfono – a telephone

una ambulancia – an ambulance

un intérprete – an interpreter

un dentista – a dentist

¿Dónde está el hospital? – Where is the hospital?

Soy alérgico/a a la penicilina – I'm allergic to penicillin

Soy… – I'm…

diabético/a – diabetic

asmático/a – asthmatic

Me duele aquí – It hurts here

Creo que está roto – I think it's broken

Necesito… – I need…

dentífrico – toothpaste

paracetamol – paracetamol

Tengo una receta de mi médico – I've got a prescription here from the doctor

¿Tiene algo para…? – Have you got anything for…?

dolor de garganta – a sore throat

la tos – a cough

pie de atleta – athlete's foot

¿Puede recomendar algo para un resfrío? – Can you recommend anything for a cold?

Tengo… – I'm suffering from…

alergia al polen – hay fever

indigestión – indigestion

diarrea – diarrhoea

un sarpullido – a rash

Puede probar esta crema – You could try this cream

Si no se pasa en una semana, debería ver a un médico – If it doesn't clear up after a week, you should see your doctor

¿Puedo comprar esto sin receta? – Can I buy this without a prescription?

Solo está disponible con receta – It's only available on prescription

¿Tiene efectos secundarios? – Does it have any side effects?

Debe evitar el alcohol – You should avoid alcohol

Necesito ver a un médico – I'd like to see a doctor

¿Tiene cita? – Do you have an appointment?

¿Es urgente? – Is it urgent?

Me gustaría hacer una cita para ver al/a la Dr… – I'd like to make an appointment to see Dr…

¿Hay doctores que hablen…? – Are there any doctors who speak…?

¿Tiene seguro médico? – Do you have private medical insurance?

Por favor, tome asiento – Please, take a seat

El doctor está listo para verlo/a – The doctor's ready to see you now

¿Cómo puedo ayudarlo/a? – How can I help you?

¿Cuál es el problema? – What's the problem?

¿Cuáles son los síntomas? – What are your symptoms?

Tengo… – I've got a…

una fiebre – temperature

dolor de garganta – sore throat

dolor de cabeza – headache

un sarpullido – a rash

Me siento enfermo/a – I've been feeling sick

Estoy muy congestionado/a – I'm very congested

Tengo diarrea – I've got diarrhea

Estoy constipado/a – I'm constipated

Tengo un bulto – I've got a bump

Tengo un tobillo hinchado – I've got a swollen ankle

Me duele mucho – I'm in a lot of pain

Me duele… – I've got a pain in my…

la espalda – back

el pecho – chest

Necesito… – I need…

otro inhalador – another inhaler

más insulina – some more insulin

me cuesta respirar – I'm having difficulty breathing

Tengo poca energía – I've got very little energy

Me siento muy cansado – I've been feeling very tired

Me cuesta dormir – I've been having difficulty sleeping

¿Hace cuánto tiempo se siente así? – How long have you been feeling like this?

¿Puede ser que esté embarazada? – Is there any possibility you might be pregnant?

¿Tiene alergias? – Do you have any allergies?

Soy alérgico/a a los antibióticos – I'm allergic to antibiotics

¿Toma algún medicamento? – Are you on any sort of medication?

¿Dónde duele? – Where does it hurt?

Me duele aquí – It hurts here

¿Duele cuando toco aquí? – Does it hurt when I press here?

Voy a tomar su... – I'm going to take your...

presión – blood pressure

temperatura – temperature

pulso – pulse

Su presión es... – Your blood pressure is...

bastante baja – quite low

normal – normal

bastante alta – rather high

muy alta – very high

Su temperatura es... – Your temperature's...

normal – normal

un poco alta – a little high

muy alta – very high

Abra su boca, por favor – Open your mouth, please

Tosa, por favor – Cough, please

Necesitará un par de puntos – You're going to need a few stitches

Le pondré una inyección – I'm going to give you an injection

Necesitamos... – We need...

una muestra de orina – urine sample

una muestra de sangre – blood sample

Necesitamos hacerle un análisis de sangre – You need to have a blood test

Le voy a recetar antibióticos – I'm going to prescribe you some antibiotics

Tome dos de estas píldoras/pastillas tres veces al día – Take two of these pills three times a day

¿Fuma? – Do you smoke?

Debe dejar de fumar – You should stop smoking

¿Cuánto alcohol bebe por semana? – How much alcohol do you drink a week?

Debería beber menos – You should cut down on your drinking

Necesita perder peso – You need to try and lose some weight

antiséptico – antiseptic

aspirina – aspirin

talco – foot powder

vendas/banditas/curitas – bandages

jarabe para la tos – cough mixture

anticonceptivos de emergencia – emergency contraception

gotas para los ojos – eye drops

un equipo de primeros auxilios – first aid kit

laxantes – laxatives

medicina – medicine

analgésicos – painkillers

paracetamol – paracetamol

prueba de embarazo – pregnancy test

receta – prescription

pastillas para dormir – sleeping tablets

termómetro – thermometer

pañuelos – tissues

vitaminas – vitamins

preservativos/condones – condoms

pañales – diapers/nappies

termo – hot water bottle

protector/loción solar – sun cream

mejilla – cheek

mentón – chin

cabeza – head

cabello – hair

oreja/oído – ear

ojo – eye

ceja – eyebrow

pestaña – eyelash

párpado – eyelid

frente – forehead

mandíbula – jaw

labio – lip

boca – mouth

nariz – nose

lengua – tongue

diente – tooth

brazo – arm

axila – armpit

espalda – back

seno – breast

pecho – chest

codo – elbow

mano – hand

dedo – finger/toe

uña – fingernail/toenail

cuello – neck

hombro – shoulder

garganta – throat

cintura – waist

muñeca – wrist

tobillo – ankle

ano – anus

vientre – belly

nalgas – buttocks

pie – foot

genitales – genitals

cadera – hip

rodilla – knee

pierna – leg

apéndice – appendix

vejiga – bladder

cerebro – brain

corazón – heart

intestinos – intestines

riñones – kidneys

hígado – liver

pulmones – lungs

esófago – oesophagus

órgano – organ

estómago – stomach

vena – vein

costilla – rib

esqueleto – skeleton

cráneo – skull

columna vertebral – spine

sangre – blood

flema – phlegm

saliva – saliva

sudor – sweat

lágrimas – tears

orina – urine

vómito – vomit

hueso – bone

articulación – joint

músculo – muscle

nervio – nerve

piel – skin

respirar – to breathe

llorar – to cry

estornudar – to sneeze

sudar – to sweat

orinar – to urinate

vomitar – to vomit

ver – to see

oír – to hear

oler – to smell

peine – comb

acondicionador/crema de enjuague – conditioner

hilo dental – dental floss

desodorante – deodorant

cepillo – hairbrush

enjuague bucal – mouthwash

alicate – nail scissors

perfume – perfume

navaja/máquina de afeitar/afeitadora – razor

toallas femeninas – sanitary towels

champú/shampoo – shampoo

jabón – soap

tampones – tampons

cepillo de dientes – toothbrush

dentífrico – toothpaste

pinza – tweezers

algodón – cotton wool

delineador – eyeliner

sombra para ojos – eyeshadow

base – foundation

tintura para el cabello – hair dye

gel para el cabello – hair gel

crema de manos – hand cream

lapiz labial – lipstick

maquillaje – makeup

crema humectante – moisturising cream

Important terms

laptop – laptop

tableta digital – tablet

pantalla – screen

teclado – keyboard

impresora – printer

cable – cord

disco duro – hard drive

parlantes – speakers

cable de alimentación – power cord

correo electrónico/email – email

aplicación – app

cargador – phone charger

dirección de correo electrónico – email address

usuario – username

contraseña – password

responder – to reply

reenviar – to forward

nuevo mensaje – new message

archivo adjunto – attachment

enchufar – to plug in

desenchufar – to unplug

encender – to switch on

apagar – to switch off

reiniciar – to restart

internet – internet

sitio web – website

Wi-Fi – Wi-Fi

descargar – to download

archivo – file

carpeta – folder

documento – document

iniciar sesión – to log in

cerrar sesión – to log out

memoria – memory

imprimir – to print

Manufactured by Amazon.ca
Bolton, ON

29458342R00169